Tales
from a Far-Off
Place Called
HOME

Tales
from a Far-Off
Place Called
HOME

D. E. HENDRIX

ARPress
ILLUMINATING IDEAS,
EMPOWERING VOICES

ARPress
45 Dan Road Suite 5
Canton MA 02021

Hotline: 1(888) 821-0229
Fax: 1(508) 545-7580

Ordering Information:
Quantity sales. Special discounts are available on quantity purchases by corporations, associations, and others. For details, contact the publisher at the address above.

Printed in the United States of America.

ISBN-13:	Softcover	979-8-89389-984-9
	Hardcover	979-8-89389-985-6
	eBook	979-8-89389-983-2

Library of Congress Control Number: 2024918471

Contents

Prelude — I Do

Moist heat hangs in the Georgia air, as the congregation fans itself while the evening celebrations begin. Hickshaw's festivities are a private but public affair. Privately, each attendee has his or her own suspicions about the nuptials, but everyone holds the same public countenance of well-wishing. May, for many of the families in Hickshaw, is a time when the young choose matrimonial union, and every married woman sitting under the old, great live oak revisits the time in her life when she was the center of attention, when she wore a white dress and heralded in the beginning of a new life.

On this particular evening, church bells ring as Shirley Carmichael and Mave Michealson move toward their usual spot under the live oak near the other ladies. While about the millionth they both attended, this wedding is as exciting as the first they witnessed. The day is overcast with a touch of dew in the air as nature prepared its inhabitants for an evening shower. The two women, lifelong friends, take their spots in the late day shade while waiting for their husbands, Jamie and Gus, and the other town's men to erect tents for the evening's reception. Regardless of the number of brides that wed in this town, all the married women, old and young,

find themselves under the same live oak thinking the same thoughts, having the same feelings. For Shirley, thethoughts are of escape during a wet, humid night just after graduation, and for Mave, the thoughts are of a long-ago shotgun wedding.

Chapter One—May 1965

The smell of pine was what Shirley really remembers of that night. Connected to the woods and the forest as a child, Shirley loved nature and all that nature shared. Sometimes after a good rain she would stand in the middle of the forest behind her home and smell the oak in the dew and the pungent odor of wet dirt. If she was not helping Mave pick vegetables from the garden and then aiding with the other chores Mave was assigned, Shirley found herself down by the creek with Jamie, Gus, and some of the other boys from school, playing, talking, and kicking dirt around. Always a rough and tumble girl, Shirley surprised only her parents when she decided to abscond with Jamie for a life of adventure in the military. Her nerves a wreck and with a small backpack slung over her shoulder, she waited in the bushes behind the church in anticipation of seeing Mave on her wedding night.

Ever since childhood, Shirley and Mave made this nook behind the church a playground after services. After morning services, the Sunday school gang ignored their parents' admonitions to stay clean and they played, getting the red clay dirt that characterized Hickshaw's landscape all over them as their diversion overcame commonsense. Too afraid to actually go into the church the night of Mave's wedding, Shirley stood on the brick under one of the windows of the church while waiting for her friend and watching Mave take her vows. She wanted to catapult herself into the church to grab her friend, to beg her to please not tie herself to another human being in this way. She would have gone in there if it had not been for her own troubles. Instead, from the window, she watched Mave's bottom lip quiver, as her friend repeated the preacher's vows to Gus, her soon-to-be husband.

Mave was a contradiction of sorts, at least to Shirley. Mave and Shirley had been best friends since the sandbox, but Shirley, in this moment, did not really understand how someone could be so smart and so good, but feel so badly about not asking for what Shirley felt was Mave's natural right—her freedom. In high school, Mave was the only one who could honestly say she regularly participated in community service upon graduation, even though she hated that the two hours every Monday afternoon over at the old folks' home cut into her time with Gus and Shirley. Everyone else filled in the community services register handed out in life skills, forging the supervisors' signature and not worrying about being caught, but dutiful Mave insisted on being righteous, being good, and being honest about her community hours.

Up to this point, Shirley did not quite believe that Mave was getting married for all Mave's talk of going to college. Upon graduation, Mave had not only secured quite comfortably the honor of the valedictorian, but she also had garnered three scholarships totaling $7,500. If Mave was not at the library studying, she was in one of three extracurricular clubs she held office in at the school. However, when Mave spoke at the senior breakfast, she tripped over her words of encouragement and guidance because her thoughts were of the small child growing inside her. Standing before her graduating class, Mave could only focus on Shirley, the only soul beside Gus who knew the exact trajectory her life would take—motherhood.

These thoughts consumed Shirley as she watched Mave finish her vows. When the preacher asked for objections from the crowd, Shirley hoped and prayed that someone would be courageous and speak up in Mave's defense and speak up against the marriage. As Mave made her final vow, Shirley's stomach and heart sank. Afterward, Shirley watched Mave's in-laws embrace her. Minutes later, Mave found peace and solitude on the porch of the church, but even this peace would be interrupted by Shirley's quiet whisper in the dark. Mave looked over the railing and then stepped off the porch to speak to Shirley, to beg her not to leave Hickshaw.

"Shirley, are ya sure ya can't stay even until the reception's over?" Mave asked.

"I wanna stay, but tonight's my only night. Jamie's leavin'. He's my only ride. It's the only time my parents will be gone." Shirley continued, "Sure ya don't wanna to come? Plenty of women have babies and go to school, Mave."

"I can't. I'm already married, Shirley," Mave answered, a hint of melancholy in her voice.

Shirley paused and then stated flatly, "Mave, ya don't havta stay married."

For Shirley, the ceremony's importance was an obstacle Mave needed to traverse, but the commitment Mave made to Gus had not set in with Shirley until she spoke with Mave.

Missing Mave's wedding broke Shirley's heart. Missing this event almost brought her to tears at moments, as she would miss the wedding of the closest friend she had in life. Of course, Shirley wanted to attend as a maid of honor, but her only chance to leave town would be while her parents were at Mave's wedding. Mave understood the truth of Shirley's reality without ever having to speak a word to Shirley about it.

Unlike Mave, Shirley was engaged to a boy who was everything a wife could want in a husband, except Shirley did not want him or to be married to him. He could give her the life beyond what she expected only if she wanted it. Even with all of Shirley's protests that he was not the one, her parents believed they were evenly yoked, and they decided it was best she marry him. Instead of obeying her parents' wishes, she ran on the day of her best friend's wedding.

Shirley was not made of the steel that Mave was, though. Pregnancy was the death knell to an extremely smart girl on the move, and Mave was no exception. For the love and reputation of her family, Mave avoided scandal even though it pained her to sacrifice the one goal she had kept for only herself—an education. In the end, Mave resigned herself to a marriage with someone with whom teenage love and passion had been derailed by the real-life tragedy of teenage parenthood.

Mave, however, did not have to drag Gus to the altar, which was good because she was an anxious bride, anxious about everything being "in order" and "just right." The evening of the wedding, Mave had to do everything in her power to keep her nerves in check. She was about five months along, and she could feel the baby's restlessness in her womb. She loved Gus, but she was not quite sure she wanted to marry him.

Gus was raised with good people, so he knew what was expected of him. He would be a great and faithful father, never straying from her even in thought, and more importantly, he would love his children dearly.

Gus did not letter in any sport, but he could tell a million fishing stories to make a sad day smile. On the outside, some would say these two kids did not match, Mave with her Oxford sweaters, plaid skirts, penny loafers, and cat-framed glasses, while Gus drove a pickup and wore camouflage jackets to school. For Gus, school had been a chore. In fact, the only reason he attended the last few years of school was because Mave went, and he just wanted to be close to her all day. For Mave, school had been a religion.

Before the pregnancy, she earned a scholarship to the local junior college she would attend, except a baby and a husband would make it difficult to work in a college degree. Even in the midst of this setback and her own disappointment, Mave only saw Gus, the boy whom she asked to the Sadie Hawkins Dance, standing next to her wanting her hand in marriage.

Before the wedding that day, Mave stood in front of the mirror dressed in a lace and chiffon white wedding dress examining her shape. Her slightly bulging belly was concealed by a heavy veil—her mother's idea. Mave's countenance revealed an unsettledness that a mere wedding ring could not assuage. Her thoughts about her impending wedding were interrupted by her younger sister, Marla.

"Oh, you look so beautiful," swooned Marla.

"Thanks," Mave said as she swept a black curl from her face. She dabbed more rouge on her face and turned toward her little sister.

"Go tell Mama and Daddy I'm 'bout ready t'head to the church."

As her little sister hurried down the steps, almost tripping over herself, Mave lifted the gown and stepped into her mother's slightly ill-fitting, eggshell pumps.

"Ready," Mave called from the top stair. Her father, standing six foot four inches, walked up to the top stair carefully entwining his arm in hers and walking down into the hallway.

"Oh, what a sight you are, honey."

"Thanks, Daddy."

When they reached the hallway where the lights were better, her mother exclaimed, "Mave! I knew that dress would be perfect on you."

In all of the excitement, Mave's only emotions were utter discontent. No matter how beautiful the dress was or how her hair fell just right, this moment was not where she imagined she would be or where she wanted to be.

However, when Daddy walked her down the aisle toward the preacher and Gus, she could only think of years and years of marital security, family comfort, a good name, and of course, motherhood. Before she knew it, she made it permanent. "I do," Mave said in a voice so quiet she almost could not be heard.

Chapter Two — A Live Oak

"Sweetheart, where are you goin'?" asked Mrs. Johnson, a married, settled woman well into her thirties. Mrs. Johnson watched from out of the corner of her eyes as Mave walked toward a gaggle of her high school friends sitting on the perimeter of the shaded tree.

"I was just gonna sit with some friends until the tents were ready," Mave answered innocently, trying to escape the meddling mature woman. While innocent, Mave was not naïve. Mave recognized the circumstances of her wedding and did not want to even take the chance that the women of Hickshaw would ask a question that would result in a lie she did not want to tell.

"You're married now. Come sit with us."

"But," Mave began to explain. She began to move toward the friends from high school that she wanted to speak to before school let out since she knew she probably would not get to talk to them again, seeing as she would be occupied with motherhood, but Mrs. Johnson would not have it any other way.

"Won't take no for an answer," Mrs. Johnson said.

Without a word to her friends, Mave took her new spot under the oak tree with the other married women and watched Gus and the other men set up the tents. While watching the men work, Mave listened intently to the women chatter about their lives.

"Rusty's been seeing that girl over in Statesboro, and it's been drivin' his mother to madness," commented one of the women.

"I don't understand why he has'ta go all the way to 'nother city to court, especially when there are plenty a' girls here," said another.

"Well, his father did the same thing. Went into the military and come home married to that Filipina," a third chimed in.

Then there was the talk about more personal matters.

"I don't know what's gotten into him. It's like the last couple of nights he's been at me. I could barely make it to Mave's wedding. I'm so tired. Haven't had a full night's rest since last Saturday."

"Tell'm no and put'm on the couch," said another.

"Then he'll start wanderin' again, and couldn't stand for that," the woman answered.

"What is he? A dog? Put'm on the couch and tell'm to mind his manners."

When the talk could not get any worse, she found herself wanting to seek the sanctuary of her high school girlfriends, who laughed with innocence at the boys on the grounds helping with the tents. Before she could flee the group of women, Mave was shocked by another confession.

"I'm pregn'nt, again," Mary Sue Patterson announced. She had been one of Mave's mother's good friends, and one who had spent countless Saturdays at her home. She was a young woman, no older than thirty, but she seemed so much older to Mave.

"Really? That makes eight," one woman said, excited for the young woman.

"I know, but I'm thinkin' about—"

"An abortion. You can't do that," warned another woman who had sat quietly for most of the conversation.

"Haven't had a break since I was sixteen, and I'm barely shy of thirty," Mary Sue said.

"Let the older ones tend to the younger ones."

"It's still a whole lot of work. I'll figure something out."

In that time, Mave saw her future standing in front of her, daring her to protest her own circumstances.

At weddings before her own, she and the other young girls had sat far away under the hot Georgia sun and, while sitting under the hundred-year-old oak tree and listening to grown up chatter, they dreamt of being included in the mystery of married life, the secrecy of it all. For young girls and the courting and unmarried women, a spot under the oak tree was like being invited entry into a club whose membership only required a ring. The conversation on this particular day was disappointing for Mave because the only intrigue she found among this group of women was unending demands for sex, excessive children, and few, if any, moments of happiness or freedom. Mave only felt the restraints of wedded bliss lock her in place even more, and right before Mave decided to join the comfort of her high school friends the tents were ready. The women then set out southern delicacies on several long tables.

Just about the whole town turned out for the wedding because Mave was such a good girl about the situation. She and Gus became engaged when she first learned of the impending birth of her first child, both doing the right thing, the mature thing. There was never a question about what Mave would do, at least not openly. Mave decided she would not try to do it alone, nor would she run as some of the others had. Her family had a good name in town, and she was not the one to ruin it, especially when the solution was so simple.

At times during the reception, she would glance over at the Carmicheals, knowing what Shirley would do. Shirley's parents were good people, and part of Mave was angry with Shirley for ruining the Carmichaels' good name, but at the same time, she understood Shirley. The Carmichaels rose with the sun and worked hard until dusk, like everybody else in Hickshaw. They attended the same social gatherings, the glue that held the town together, and so naturally the Carmichaels shared the same views on marriage and love.

At a certain age, a girl should get herself ready to have a husband, and with Mave getting married, they thought after high school would be the most appropriate time to skip the complications of courtship and all of the worries that accompany it. In the past, common practice dictated that parents arrange a wedding for their children, especially girl children. In some circles, townspeople thought it neglect if her parents did not make sure Shirley married and married well.

Mave also found Shirley's decision to leave disturbing. She did not really understand why Shirley did not want to marry Duck Hanson. Duck came from a nice family with a solid name and a lot of money. With Duck, Shirley would already have a house, and affording a home would take a while for Mave and Gus. As far as Mave was concerned, Shirley got a great deal. Plus, Duck was not too bad to look at either. When Shirley told her the news of her impending engagement some weeks before Mave's own wedding, Mave said, "You won't have any problems gettin' material for a white dress."

"Ah, don't say that. There's nothin' that says you can't wear white, honey. Yer gettin' married before the baby is born to the man what gave it to you," Shirley said.

"I know, but it don't feel quite right. Momma's gonna lend me her dress, but even then, it don't even feel right. It's like I cheated."

Shirley thought about it, and then said, "I'm thinkin' of leavin' though."

"What? Are you out of your mind, Shirley Carmichael?" Mave asked and then said, "You aren't even into boys that much. I understand."

"Yes, I am!"

"No, no yer not. You've never had a boy."

"Have so. Kissed Jamie."

"Jamie Wilkerson. Yeah right, we all know what kinda girls he likes. Don't lie, Shirley."

Realizing she would not be able to convince Mave that she and Jamie had kissed, she said, "Well, I'm not that way if that's what you're implyin'."

"No. Didn't mean it that way. I just never seen you with anyone. I'm surprised that you even agreed t'marry."

"I'm goin' into the military with Jamie."

"What? You two gettin' together? You and Jamie haven't done anything I should know about?" Mave asked.

"No, it's just an option."

"Mmm."

"Well, Mave, it's better'n sittin' around here waitin' for life to come and find me. Plus, I don't think I wanna sit 'round Hickshaw for the rest of my life." Shirley continued, "There has gotta be somethin' better'n this out there."

"When did you come to this conclusion?" Mave asked.

"I didn't come to any conclusion. Mave, seriously—I don't wanna get married."

Both of the girls sat quietly, and then Mave asked, "What's gonna become of us?"

"Oh, Mave, I can write to you. We do have phones," Shirley said.

"Yeah, but it's awful expensive to call long distance."

"A stamp is a quarter. We'll write to each other."

The last Mave would hear of Shirley before the Carmichaels discovered Shirley left was right after she and Gus took their vows. Mave sat in front of the awning talking when she heard a hushed voice from behind the porch. Shirley was out of place among the wedding guests. She wore a T-shirt with a Coke logo on it, jeans, and tennis shoes. Mave was so deep in conversation with the other girls regarding their plans for after June that she almost did not hear Shirley. Mave just happened to look in the direction of the bushes where she saw her friend standing behind the railing.

"Shirley, you came!" Mave exclaimed.

"Shh. I don't want my parents to know I'm here. Remember, I'm supposed to be in bed," Shirley said. "You look so beautiful. Come here." She pulled her friend into an embrace she would not feel again until years after this conversation.

"Where's Jamie?" Mave asked.

"He's in the truck. I only got a few minutes. I wanna give you this," Shirley said.

Shirley pulled a small burgundy box out of her purse. A gold ring with a topaz setting was in the box. At first, Mave looked confused because the ring was the type found in a bubble gum machine.

"I know. I wanted to give you somethin'. I can't really afford it just yet. They said we're supposed to give somethin' blue, and this is all I had," Shirley said.

"Oh," Mave said, the reality of Shirley leaving finally hitting her. She said, "I really wish you did not have to go, at least not like this."

"I can't get married. Not to him, not right now. I'm not ready," Shirley said.

Mave did not even attempt to get her friend to back down, especially after the day she had. Up there at the altar, getting married seemed right, but while under the live oak with the other women, she felt just the opposite.

Because of her own ambivalence about marriage, Mave only reached out her hand to Shirley and said, "If you need anythin' at all, just write."

"I know," Shirley said. "I gotta go."

Shirley then turned but not before hearing Mave yell behind her in the dark, "Don't be afraid to come home, Shirley Carmichael!" Shirley then disappeared into the blackness of that May evening.

Chapter Three — Freedom

The Carmichaels returned from Mave's wedding happy and in anticipation of Shirley's trip down the aisle. Mrs. Carmichael could not wait because Mave would marry and leave Shirley by herself, at least for a while. Shirley's mother could not bear the thought of watching Mave and her new family and having to field questions about the lack of domesticity in her own daughter's life. This competition between Mave and Shirley's mother always existed but only increased as the girls developed, and Mave's mother had no idea she and her daughter were participants. When Mave made honor roll, Eveline got on Shirley about her grades. Mave got her first job, and Shirley soon followed, both of them flipping burgers side by side at Patsy's. When Eveline and her husband opened the door and found a note sitting on the kitchen table explaining Shirley's absence, the anxiety that registered on Eveline's face was too hard for her husband to watch because he recognized that Mrs. Carmichael would have to explain to the whole town why a summer wedding would not take place for Carmichaels.

"I love you, but I don't wanna get married," were the last words her husband uttered to his wife on behalf of Shirley in the stillness of the midnight.

Eveline and Jody Carmichael sat across from each other, the

former close to tears while the latter sat stern-faced, only a stitch in the brow indicating the tumult inside. The next morning, the whole house was awakened by the youngest Carmichael boy announcing to his other siblings, "Shirley's gawn!"

The Carmichaels did what most in their situation would do.

"We're really sorry. We just can't talk 'bout it right now, Charles," Jody Carmichael explained to Duck's father. "But as soon as we can, we'll let ya know." He continued to talk to Duck's father, reassuring him that the problem was not on their part, and Mrs. Carmichael stood in the background searching Jody's face for any indication of Hanson's reaction.

Hours before the news of Shirley's escape reached her parents, Shirley turned to leave Mave who stood in the tranquility of the darkness. On the way to Jamie's car, Shirley cried because she knew she probably would not see Mave and her family for a while. Wiping the tears from her eyes, Shirley saw Jamie leaning on his truck, arms folded.

"Girl, you cryin'?" Jamie asked. He continued, "Look, you don't havta come."

"Jamie. I wanna go. Let's go."

"No, listen, Shirley," he said hugging her. "I want you to be real sure you wanna come because once I start out, I have no intention of turning around."

"I said, let's go!" Shirley said with urgency, knowing she had to leave before she changed her mind and returned home and returned to her impending marriage.

Jamie was ambivalent about leaving because while he wanted out of Hickshaw Junction since his freshman year, the town had become home to him. Jamie moved to Hickshaw from Miami in middle school right after his parents separated, so he was not as attached to Hickshaw.

He eventually learned all of things that made a proper Hickshaw boy. He fished, he hunted, and he drove a truck, all built by his own hands. For all intents and purposes, Jamie was one of them, but he stood on the margins, often watching his life and those around him while wondering when he would leave that prison he built for himself.

According to town gossip, his father left his mother right before they moved to the small town. In fact, the entire reason his family moved was because of the separation. Jamie's parents did not actually divorce until some years later, but his father, Jackson Wilkerson, occasionally dropped in when things with the woman he was dating did not quite work out. His mother, Maureen, grew up in Hickshaw, so her decision to move was mainly related to her need to be around those who loved her, understood her, and could comfort her without judging her about her single lifestyle. All of these issues made life for Jamie intolerable, and so Jamie, who had grown used to the city, counted the seconds to the day that he would be able to leave Hickshaw forever.

Shirley waited by the truck while Jamie unlocked the door. He opened the car door on Shirley's side and she got in. He ran around to the front of the car, slapping the hood with his hand, excited that finally he would be leaving and beginning a new life where he was the sole person responsible for the consequences of his own actions. Both of them sat in the cab of truck and listened to Dolly Parton croon "Jolene" from the car radio.

"Whatcha thinkin' about?" Jamie asked.

"Oh, nothin' really. Just on life," Shirley said in a reflective tone.

"Well, what about life?"

"I don't know. Seeing Mave all dressed up in that weddin' gown made me think. 'Damn,' Jamie, 'We're adults.'"

"Did she look nice?"

"Oh, she was beautiful. Remember Homecomin'?"

"Yep."

"She was hundred times as beautiful."

"And probably a thousand times as miserable," Jamie said sardonically. He then asked, "Is the baby showing yet?"

"Yep. Just a little," she said. Jamie was not supposed to know Mave was pregnant, except Shirley accidentally told him as they walked home from school one day.

"Shirley."

"What?"

"Can I ask you something?'"

"Sure."

"Why did you even say yes to that boy if you knew you didn't want to marry at all, much less marry him?"

Shirley sat quietly for a minute and then said, "At first I was surprised. Me and Duck been in school together since we were little. He use'ta spend a lot of time at our house. Our parents are close. I guess I just thought it was natural we'd get married."

Shirley stopped to reflect on the moment she changed her mind. "I dunno. Actually, I do. You remember Rebecca?"

"Yep. She left last year. Supposed be livin' in sin with a guy she met at work," Jamie said sarcastically.

She continued, "Yeh. Well, I saw her a couple weeks ago, and she hasn't done too badly fer herself."

"Really."

"Yeh. She's goin' to college and sounds like the boy's real nice."

"You'd a thought with all the talk she'd committed some crime," Jamie added.

"I know. That's my point, Jamie." Shirley continued. "It's like people 'round here do what's expected and talk. They love to talk. They don't really consider someone could do just fine without bein' married."

She breathed a great sigh and said, "After seein' her, I just wanted to give myself a chance—" She trailed off. "To do somethin' different."

Shirley finished, "Duck is nice, and I suppose he would've made a great husband, just not mine."

"I can understand that," Jamie said and then took a glance at Shirley's profile. A stoplight interrupted their travel, and without notice, a feeling of total and overwhelming abandonment overcame him for the only girl he ever considered cool enough to take fishing with him. He reached across the cab's seat and quickly kissed Shirley on the cheek.

"Stop that. What are you doin', Jamie? Watch the road, will ya'?" Shirley said and wiped the wet, sticky coolness off her face.

"I dunno. Just wanted to kiss you. Calm down. It's not like I'm askin' to marry ya'," he said jokingly and then added, "Shoot, I'd probably have to tackle ya'. I can't believe you're runnin' from that man."

Shirley let down the car window and let the cool breeze caress her face. Their trip to Macon was a blur. As Shirley would later tell Mave, "Nothin' but blackness." Jamie continued to drive while Shirley stared out of the window. She would leave for basic training in three weeks and Jamie would leave in a week. In the meantime, they would stay with Jamie's aunt in Macon. After Jamie's departure, Shirley would help in his aunt's boutique while she waited to leave for basic training.

The whole way to Macon, the only thoughts Shirley had were of her parents and how she hurt them. She did not want to marry, and she did not want to get into arguments with her parents, especially Mother, about the pleasures of marriage. At the same time, Shirley's departure impacted her mother in a way that left her mother angry, depressed, and disappointed in her daughter, as they were extremely close, and Shirley did not need to call home to know this fact. With the impending marriage, they really seemed to see eye to eye on a lot. Shirley even went so far as to pick out material for a dress. Shirley's heart sank as she thought about how her mother would explain to the world her daughter's escape while facing the embarrassment that resulted from a willful, unruly daughter.

When Jamie and Shirley reached Macon, the plan was to hang out in Macon and then to drop Jamie off at Warner Robins.

"Make sure you call as soon as you get settled," his aunt said to Jamie as he waited outside the depot. Shirley stood in the background, not sure if it was okay to cry or not. She had seen Jamie every day of her life since middle school, and him getting on that bus meant yet another friendship would slip away.

For Jamie, his departure was the culmination of all the years of watching his mother date different men, listening to town gossip about these affairs, and desiring something else for himself. However, for Shirley, his departure was just another piece of her comfortable life she would discard.

"I'm really gonna miss you," Shirley said while wrapping her arms around his waist as they said goodbye to each other.

Jamie answered, "It's gonna be alright." Then, he whispered in her ear, "You'll be glad you left. Trust me on that. I'll write to ya. I promise."

Jamie then picked up his backpack and got on the bus while his aunt and best friend watched from the terminal window at the bus depot. Shirley thought to herself, "I hope he is right," and followed his aunt to the car.

Chapter Four — Silks and Garments

Money is a means to an ends," said Ms. Charmaine.

"A what?" Shirley asked.

"A means to an end."

"What do you mean?"

"Don't get too wrapped up in money. It's fleeting. It meets most of our basic needs, but it's not the end all," Ms. Charmaine of Charmaine's Fine Silks and Garments explained.

"I don't wanna get married justa havta rely on someone else t'support me, and when I get to be where I'm makin' lots of money, I'll be able t'do whatever I want, and it won't matter that I ain't married," Shirley said innocently, right before Ms. Charmaine launched into another lecture about money.

Working in the store, Shirley watched Jamie's aunt tailor dresses for the fine, wealthy women of Macon. The talk in the shop was not too different from home, but the women were. These women spent money on themselves and it showed, and there was Ms. Charmaine in the middle of it. One day, Lacy Caravecci drove up in a late model Jaguar, and Shirley just about fell all over herself. Lacy was married to some Italian magnet, and she spent most of her summers in Italy. When the fall came, she and her brood would come back to Macon to settle for the year.

"Girl, git away from that window before you scare off my clients," said Ms. Charmaine, as the well-dressed Lacy entered the store, her bangled wrists clanging while she opened the door. While Shirley was in awe by Lacy's flashy clothes and jewels, Ms. Charmaine seemed unmoved.

"I just need the hem in this vest fixed," Lacy said and then turned in the other direction to yell at one of her children. "Tommy, stop runnin' in Ms. Charmaine's boutique!"

Lacy turned back around to face Charmaine and then explained, "I bought it in Europe last summer and didn't notice the damage."

Ms. Charmaine examined the vest and said, "I'll have it back to ya in a week."

"All right, thanks, Ms. Charmaine," Lacy explained and sailed out the door.

When Lacy was out of earshot and sight, Ms. Charmaine said, "You see that woman."

"Yep," Shirley said while still watching Lacy drive away.

"She probably spent a couple hundred dollars on that designer Italian leather vest."

Shirley interrupted, "I wonder how much she spent on those fancy wheels."

"Too much, if ya ask me. That's why you don't let money warp your perception of common sense." She continued, "That woman has almost paid for my house comin' in here havin' this and that fixed."

"But isn't that what you want?" Shirley asked.

"Hush. The point I'm tryin' to make is just because you see someone who appears to be wealthy does not mean they have sense. Money is just a means to an end. Remember that gal. A means to an end."

Three weeks later, when Ms. Charmaine of Macon, Georgia, dropped Shirley off at the same bus depot she had for her nephew a few weeks earlier, she handed Shirley a package.

"I made you somethin' you'll need in your travels," Ms. Charmaine said.

Shirley opened the package, and in the box was her first professional business suit. Not quite knowing when she would use it, she slowly placed the suit back in the box and said, "Thanks a lot. I mean—for everything." Shirley then climbed aboard the Trailways bus ready for her own adventure.

Chapter Five — A Life Deferred

As Mave's stomach became more rotund, she seemed to be constantly aware of the pressures regarding motherhood, and her mother's constant nagging only made her anxieties worse.

"Sit up, gal," her mother reminded her. "It's not good for the baby."

"Momma, what on earth does me slouchin' havta to do with havin' a baby?"

"Just sit up," Mrs. Michaelson said. Slouching just felt better. At least it took a load off her back.

"Mave."

"What, Momma?"

"Did you eat the rest of that pie?"

"Yes, I'm starvin'."

"Honey, that much sugar is not good for a baby."

"Momma, be serious. I can't starve myself. Plus, the baby won't know any better."

Mave continued to eat sugar nonstop. This back and forth between her and her mother continued throughout the summer. After a while, Mave had grown to love being a mother, even though she did not really know what to expect from motherhood. Worse yet, she did not really have anyone, other than Shirley, with whom she could share her feelings without being made to feel guilty or selfish, and Shirley was gone. Mave had not seen Shirley in three months, and Mave wanted to come out of her skin because the summer was hot, humid, and wet, and Chet hung low in her tummy. To say summer was miserable for Mave was putting it mildly. She and Gus seemed to be getting along fine, but she was still having a tough time adjusting to marriage and marital duties. The night of their wedding had been wonderful, her sitting on the edge of the bed in the trailer both sets of parents bought as a wedding gift and him getting himself ready for bed.

"So, Shirley really left?" Gus asked.

"Yep. I don't think anything could have kept her here," Mave said.

"She's always been a wild one."

"No, Gus, she hasn't been," Mave said defensively. "I think with all the excitement of the wedding she may have gotten spooked. Shirley has always been obedient."

"Okay, Mave, but I've lived in this town just as long as you. I've seen a thing or two. That girl is wild," he said as a vision of Shirley kissing Jamie by the creek after school flashed before his eyes. Mave shot him a nasty look because he was always making snide remarks about Shirley.

Seeing Mave's attitude change, he came over to the bed and said, "Honey, I don't want to argue about anything, much less about Shirley."

Gus sat down on the bed next to his wife, touching her stomach and rubbing the roundness, and lifting her hair while nuzzling the back of her neck. Mave's stiffened neck loosened as his kisses reminded her of a time when she was not so full with child.

After making love, Gus told her, "I don't wanna ever fight about other people. I love you. Don't you know that?"

She thought to herself, "Well, maybe this marriage thing wouldn't be so bad."

Marriage was not bad, except she never expected to be a homemaker the summer after she graduated from high school. Some days when Gus laid tiles with his father, she went to an old hangout, the local pool. Tightness in her chest overcame her when she saw her classmates in their bikinis while their skinny, lithe bodies frolicked in the July sun. The young women sipped on their Tabs through multicolored straws while she wore maternity wear and drank water to stave off the heat. Mave never said a word to the girls at the pool, only glancing at them and walking by as if the pool was on the way to whatever errand she had. She imagined Gus out there with her watching the young women and him loving them with his eyes, and she became very angry, jealous, and afraid that he would leave her. She would try to love him more.

The most difficult part of this entire situation was school. She kept the award certificate the high school gave her during the ceremony the previous December in the same chest as the topaz bubble gum ring Shirley gave her. Every now and then, she would get the courage to approach Gus about maybe taking a course or two, and they would have the same tepid conversation.

"Gus, ya know, I've been thinkin'," she said. He sat at the kitchen table eating the meatloaf, mashed potatoes, and green beans she had prepared.

"I'm here all day doin' nothin'," she continued. "I could be preparin' for a trade."

"You wanna job?" he asked, slowly chewing his food, his right eyebrow raised.

Mave sat across from him running her finger across the flowered tablecloth her mother gave to them. She had rationalized all of the reasons why she should go to school and she was ready for him.

Her first reason was, "I could help bring some money into the house if I went to school and got a trade."

"Mave, I don't think that's such a good idea with the baby comin' and all."

"It wouldn't hurt for me to enroll in a few courses. Just so if I wanna work I'll at least have some classes under my belt," she blurted out. She tried to get him to concede. "Gus, the scholarship is still good."

"We'll see when the baby gets here," he said, and then he continued, "Go turn down the bed sheet."

Mave got up from the table, placed the hand towel she used to dry the dishes on the hook in the kitchen, and walked back toward the bedroom. The little hallway engulfed and enclosed her in a claustrophobic cell. She took small breaths, trying to recollect herself. Deep inside, she knew there would be no schooling, at least not in the near future, so she put it aside the same way she had put aside many of the plans she had for her future that year. As she felt the walls close in on her, she walked to the bedroom and then turned down the bed sheet.

Chapter Six — Departures

Jamie got on the bus feeling as though this departure would be the cure for his life. At the same time, he looked at Shirley and his aunt as the bus pulled away from the station and knew he was leaving a part of himself in that depot. Ever since his father's departure, everything he had become was in Hickshaw. His mother tried, but even with her stable boyfriends, she was never quite able to negate the impact Jamie's father's absence had on him. His mother's boyfriends were nice men who taught him how to change the oil in the car, took him to his baseball games, and even counseled his mother when Jamie racked up a string of girlfriends. Nevertheless, these relationships were temporary, and each man soon was replaced by someone Maureen deemed more exciting, more interesting.

Like his mother, Jamie found dating exhilarating. Every now and then, one of the fathers of the girls he dated would get on the phone with his mother to discuss his concerns about Jamie's reputation. Most of the time, his mother would invite the father over to dinner and then, well, they would talk. Jamie was accustomed to a new place setting once in a while when these occasions occurred. Afterward, Jamie would go to his room and close his door, knowing what his mother and somebody's father would engage in. Some of the men stuck around shortly after, and some stuck around for a while longer.

Johansson stuck around a long while after dinner with his mother. Clara Johansson was a girl Jamie dated for about three months. Of any the girls he dated, she was closest he ever came to falling in love. When he broke her heart, her father Billy showed up at his mother's modest home to get an explanation.

"Mr. Johansson, Jamie is a good boy raised with good morals," she said slightly apologetically while Jamie shifted from one foot to another waiting for the moment when he could leave.

"Jamie, come over here and say hello to Mr. Johansson," his mother said. Jamie walked over to the place where his mother and Johansson stood and shook the hand of the man who would be a surrogate father for a while. Johansson already knew Jamie had sex with his daughter. The father just wanted Jamie to know of his presence in his daughter's life and that he would not allow Jamie to play with her. Once Johansson extended his hand, Jamie shook it just as his father had told him to do. Jamie's father explained to him the art of the handshake one afternoon before he introduced his son to a few of his lawyer buddies.

"Don't squeeze. The handshake should be firm but not enough to hurt the fella."

Jamie did not really care about what people in town thought of his divorcee mother because, to him, they were all hypocrites. For some reason, though, on this day while he rode away to his new life, Johansson remained stuck in his mind, maybe because he was one of the ones who did not leave his mother by herself on her birthday or on Valentine's Day. When the Johansson's Oldsmobile rolled up to the house on these holidays, Jamie often wondered how Johansson could leave his wife on such important days, and when Johansson and his mother went away to Vegas for two weeks, Jamie thought he actually might have a stepfather. By this time, Johansson's daughter had been out of the picture for Jamie, and Johansson and Jamie's mom were talking about actually making a life together after Johansson left his

28

wife, but he first had to leave his wife.

Jamie was scared for his mother because the memory of his father's abandonment and the hope that his father would reunite with his family remained etched in his psyche. The four of them—him, his mother and his two sisters—had some hard times trying to extricate his father from their lives. When Johansson seemed to be a permanent fixture in his mother's life, he worried because the other men had played with her. Even though he was angry with his mother for many reasons, he did not want to see her brokenhearted.

Johansson knew the deal with the kid, and he did not try to father Jamie. Girls already being a sensitive subject for both Jamie and Johansson, they never discussed the subject. The one conversation he did have with Johansson about a girl was about Shirley.

"Why don't cha ask her out?" Johansson suggested.

"Well, she's really a friend. She's not really someone you would date—like that," Jamie said forgetting about Johansson's daughter. Jamie said quickly, "I'm sorry. I didn't mean that."

Johansson stared blankly at Jamie, slightly angry but very aware of the complications of his own circumstance.

"Anyway, I'll ignore that last comment," Johansson said seriously.

Then he added, "Well, son, if she's your friend, it shouldn't be that difficult to ask her out."

Jamie looked back at the older man. He hated when his mother's men called him son.

Jamie then said, "I know. I just worry that she is too immature to deal with, you know. I have expectations—"

"Boy, you're sixteen. What on Earth would you be expect'n?"

"Actually, seventeen."

"Okay, seventeen."

They sat there silently for about a second or so when Johansson finally said, "If the girl is a nice girl, then she'll meet all of your expectations."

"She's nice, and actually we have a lot to talk about but—"

Johansson said, "I know. We probably shouldn't be havin' this conversation, but you don't want to be that person to that many girls."

Johansson got up from the porch and left Jamie to ponder exactly what he meant. Jamie did not know why he asked Johansson about Shirley, but there was a sense of decency about the guy that he had not found in any of the other men his mother dated.

The night before he left for basic training, he did get a chance to have that talk with Shirley about a relationship. He and Shirley were minding the shop and talking about old friends from school.

"How come you didn't have boyfriends in school?" Jamie asked.

"Ah, Jamie. I dunno. The opportunity never presented itself."

"Well, was there anyone that you ever liked?"

"Not really," Shirley said, but she lied. She was in love with Jamie, but he had so many girlfriends. He could not see past them to see her.

Shirley had a crush on Jamie at the end of eleventh grade. The two had been spending a lot of time together studying because he did not pass history the previous semester and would have to attend summer school at the college to get his credits for that year. To avoid having to spend his summer in one of the portables designated for high school students, every day except Fridays he studied after school with Shirley and Mave. He liked Shirley, and when they walked home together, he found they had a lot in common. They both disliked school, except Shirley at least attempted to push herself academically, and of course they had an intense love of the outdoors. Shirley was kind of scared of Jamie, seeing his mother was divorced, and with his reputation, no self-respecting girl would be seen with him alone. Even with that, they became close, and he never tried to kiss her seriously, so she did not see herself as a serious love interest. This day, though, she playfully said after a couple of quiet moments, "You were taken."

Jamie did not say anything for a minute, and then he said, "For real? Shirley, why didn't you say anything? I mean, I felt the same too, but I thought—"

"I wasn't old enough, doin' the same things," Shirley said.

"Yeah," he said.

Jamie walked over to where her head lay on the counter, and he looked at her seriously. She stood in front of him, a head shorter than him, waiting for him to kiss her. Before he could kiss her, Ms. Charmaine interrupted the pair.

"Boys and girls, I'm goin' t'bingo tonight, so you'll have to fend fer yourselves as far dinner is concerned," Aunt Charmaine said as she swung the doors of the shop open. The two kids looked surprised.

Jamie said to Shirley, "You wanna get a pizza? It's the last night we'll be together."

"Sure, just as long as you don't ask me to marry ya."

Jamie sat on the bus watching it pull away from the one girl he was actually interested in, wondering whether he would ever see her as a woman or if he would ever see her again.

Despite his misgivings and him missing Shirley, Jamie found the military to be a pleasant change. Where the people in Hickshaw only expected so much from the young man, his sergeants demanded excellence. What surprised Jamie was that he could rise to the challenge. To say that Jamie excelled in basic training would be an understatement. Every time he was taught a new skill, such as making his bed or cleaning his gun, he picked it up quickly, and then he watched as the other scrubs struggled and sometimes failed.

As someone who was at first anxious and unwilling to go into the military, Jamie found military life very comfortable. For one, there was a lot of structure. Jamie did not really understand what it meant to go to bed and wake up on a routine schedule. In Hickshaw, Jamie went to sleep when he could no longer keep his eyes open and awoke to the smell of his mother's coffee pot emitting aromas in the early hours of any morning. His mother worked long hours plucking chickens at a chicken plantation outside of Macon. By the time she got home, she would not feel like cooking, so one of his sisters cooked. When his sisters married, he either ate with them or made a sandwich. Breakfast and lunch ran in the same manner. He ate when he was hungry and not at any particular time. In the military, he ate his three squares at the chow hall at a specific time. On his first night on post, he found the dorm to be institutional and cold. By the third week, he realized when it was time to move on he would miss the regimented, disciplined routine of it all.

"Don't smile. Just set still and we'll have ya taken care of in a minute," the photographer said to Jamie just before he snapped the photo.

His sergeants made them dress in their blues for the pictures, which made him look especially dashing. He hoped he would have the chance to send one to his mother before he left for tech school. When he got the photo he looked at it, amazed by the transformation. For the first time since he was in high school, he looked sharp, clean cut even, like a man ready to take on his world. The face that stared back at him instilled in him a sense of pride. All of the skills and lessons he mastered in those few weeks were apparent on his countenance, which said, "I can be anything I want. Dare me!"

The last time he felt this way was in eighth grade. He had to argue, as a part of a debate, for the colored seating in the movie theater, which was a sensitive topic in Hickshaw at the time. Jamie did not see anything wrong with moving the colored from the balcony seating into the rows on the ground in the white section, which was closer to the screen. Jamie figured that coloreds were only interested in being entertained like most whites.

His portion of the debate started with a little story about the color of money and how it did not change because of the person's race. Then, he went on to discuss the economics of allowing the races to mix, arguing that on some nights the theater owners would be able to "pack them in, both colored and white," which would net them lots of money. He finished with Martin Luther King's historic opening, reinforcing the idea of making the world a good, safe place for all races and creeds.

By the end of the school day that same day, Jamie, who had only been in Hickshaw a year, made friends with Shirley, Mave, Gus, and some of the other more popular kids in Hickshaw. The debate made him feel so invincible that day, and since that day, there has not been another in which the burdens of life have not made him weary until he looked at the picture of himself. In the military, there were no gossiping hens to talk about him and his mother behind their backs, letting everyone in his world know he would amount to little because of whom he came from. All of the respect he earned in the military would be his own and not to be diminished by the actions of others. More importantly, he did not feel confusion and anxiety at being embarrassed with his mother's behavior, but instead he felt ashamed at this embarrassment. However, he could become whatever he wanted, and on this particular day, he was good. He considered sending his mother a copy of the photo to remind her of the good son she let go to live her own life.

Chapter Seven—Yes, Maam!

Standing in front of the mirror and admiring how the suit Ms. Charmaine made for her fit perfectly, Shirley did not notice the sergeant call all of the newly enlisted to attention. Instead, she admired the sharp angles of the suit and the way it flattered the little curves she had.

"What—are—you—doin?" screamed the drill sergeant, and Shirley almost jumped out of the suit.

"I—I—"

She did not have a chance to finish before Sergeant McCalister yelled, "Stand at attention!" Shirley looked around the room and saw the girls standing in front of their beds. She slipped between the sergeant and the bed and slinked into place. Standing in front of the bed, she listened as McCalister read the rules.

"You will wake at 0500 hours for PT. Lights out at 1000 hours. You get Sundays off and two Saturday afternoons a month off. You can call home once a week—"

The recruiter told her during the induction what to expect, but she thought since it was the first day, they would have a little time to get settled. However, from the moment the inductees set foot on base, they would listen to six weeks of hollering to do this or hollering to do that. She soon learned quickly there was never a right answer because the recruits were always wrong. A scrub could give the best and most articulate answer possible, but there was always a better one.

As the sergeant barked orders, she thought about Jamie, Mave, and her family, and wave of regret washed over her. Her mind raced, trying to figure a way out of this mess she created for herself. After Sarge finished, the inductees showered and went to bed. In bed that night, she thought about Jamie's words, "Trust me." Scared and anxious all at once, she calmed down enough to fall into a deep sleep, reassuring herself that her friend would not lead her astray. The stress of the day lulled her into such a deep sleep that she was startled when McCalister woke them up at 5:00 a.m. sharp beating the metal bed rails with a cane. Wiping the sleep out of her eyes and in the slow movement of bedhead tiredness, she moved to the cattle showers with the other girls. That morning they ran and ran and then ran some more. Those first couple of days their superiors were either exercising the life out of them or yelling at them. "I might actually havta fight," Shirley thought to herself as she watched McCalister put one of the troops in a chokehold.

Shirley arrived that Thursday, and she did not have a chance to speak to her bunkmates much less meet anyone. The first time they actually got a break was that Sunday. When that first Sunday arrived, the look on all of the girls' faces was of utter exhaustion. Sunday was the finish line to the marathoners, and the casualty list was long. Susy Esposito, from East LA, broke three nails that first day. Shirley's feet formed huge red blisters from the long hours in boots. Laura Angoleri, from Orlando, spent all of Saturday in the infirmary from heat exhaustion. That Sunday, the barracks was more like a convalescence home than a training camp for female soldiers, and this made the invisible fence that protected each girl from a reality other than her own come down. Shirley met two girls, Shannon Francis from Mississippi and Candace Jenkins from Georgia. The girls happened to meet while Shirley was watching them apply makeup one morning. Without thinking about it, Shirley asked her, "Why are you wearing makeup? It's so hot. Yer just gonna sweat it off."

Shannon said, "I don't intend on being in the military forever. It doesn't hurt to look good. You don't know who you might meet."

"You're trying to get married?" Candace asked.

"Why? There's nothing wrong with joining to get married. I get to have my pick of any soldier while seeing the world," Shannon stated. Candace sat on the counter next to one of the sinks and rolled her eyes.

Feeling a little defensive, Shannon asked, "So why'd you join?"

Shirley hesitated. "I didn't wanna get married."

"Huh," said Shannon while Candace sat rapt waiting for an explanation.

"My parents had me engaged to this fella. I just wasn't ready to commit like that."

The two girls sighed a collective, "Oh."

"Why did you join?" Shannon said to Candace.

"My parents threw me out of the house," Candace said. Both Shirley and Shannon looked at Candace for further clarification.

Candace then explained, "My parents found me with my boyfriend and told me I had to leave."

"You're not allowed to date?" Shirley asked, not really understanding Candace's meaning.

"They caught me, you know," Candace said and placed her tongue in her cheek, poking it out. Shirley did not know what it meant, but knew it had to be something sexual and disgusting, and so she just moved the conversation in another direction.

Of the two, Shannon and Shirley had the most in common, but

Candace fit in just fine. These girls made the five weeks that were left that much more bearable. They reminded her of home. Speaking of which, it had been about a month since she had spoken to anyone from home. She talked to Jamie briefly because he too was enduring life as a scrub. She did not garner the courage to call home until halfway through basic training and she had not thought about Hickshaw until the last week when they spent one night out in the woods in survival training.

Friday afternoon, the young women trekked five miles through the forest behind the training camp. Shirley had never wallowed in so much dirt and mud in all her life. Saturday morning, she woke up to the taste of grit in her mouth because there was so much dirt and dust everywhere. The women spent the day ducking and hiding behind trees and shrubs trying to hide from an enemy with whom they would never meet. Wilderness training was not for Shirley, as every time she heard McCalister's horn blow, she wanted to be in the warm, dry comfort of the barracks. To Shirley's dismay, she would not relax until later into the evening. After eating a ration, Shirley pitched her tent just before the first heavy rain fell that evening. Under the shelter, Shirley began to think of another day in a different forest almost a year earlier.

Shirley, Mave, Gus, Jamie, Georgette, Jack, and a few others from school were at one of the bonfires they had after attending a football game. The mild October day had cooled into a temperate evening. The bonfire was a weekly event that the kids of Hickshaw High waited in anticipation of. As usual, Mave paired up with Gus and Jaime was hanging out with Georgette, one of the high school cheerleaders. These pairings left Shirley and Jack, one the high school's most popular football players, uncomfortably sitting on a piece of wood together. Everyone sat around waiting for someone to initiate a drinking game.

"Okay, now for some serious talk—truth or dare," Gus said passing a beer to Mave.

Jack said, "Truth or dare—you first."

"Dare," Gus said.

Jack said, "I dare you to kiss Shirley—in the mouth." Before Shirley protested, Gus walked over to her.

"Oh no. you don't! Mave, come get him," Shirley exclaimed while almost falling off the wooden log. At first, Mave watched Shirley and Gus in amusement.

Then Mave said, "Leave her alone, Gus." Mave turned toward Jack and said, "Not funny. Pick somethin' else."

"Come on, Shirley. It's only a kiss," Gus said.

"Leave her alone, Gus!" Mave said. "Gus, leave her alone. Pick somethin' else Jack."

"Oh, all right. Gus, tell us what you were doin' with Ronnie behind the concession stand."

"What?" Mave asked Gus.

"That's a truth, not a dare," Gus said and then turned to Mave. "We weren't doin' nothin'."

Shirley, Jamie, Georgette, and Jack watched the beginnings of one of Mave and Gus's fights. They always fought over something, with Mave getting mad and stomping off somewhere and Gus following close behind. This time it took Mave only a couple of minutes to stomp off in the other direction while the remaining four watched the pair.

The flames were still burning when Jack turned to Shirley and looked her over. He moved closer to her, and Shirley watched him through her peripheral vision, dreading having to push him off. In the other corner, Georgette and Jamie sat with Georgette sitting in front of Jamie.

"Will you quit it?" Shirley said, annoyed by Jack's constant advances.

"Come on. Nobody's gonna care."

"I said git off me, Jack!" she said while pushing him away. Then Shirley half screamed, half cried, "Stop!" Jamie was on his feet before Jack could move away from Shirley.

"Leave her alone!" Jamie said and pushed Jack onto the ground. Jack was drunk, so when he tried to get off the ground to defend himself, Jamie just pushed him onto the ground again. Shirley flew past both of them, and Jamie followed her.

"Are you okay?" Jamie asked while hugging Shirley.

"Yeah, I'm fine," she said, her voice filled with anxiety. "I just don't wanna make out with him." She then asked, "Why did you guys invite him?"

"I didn't. Mave did." Then he added, "You don't have to go back there if you don't want."

"I know, Jamie. I'll be all right."

The two walked back to the camp fire, where Mave and Gus had already returned. Mave looked at Shirley with such disappointment. Shirley and Mave had done everything together except double date. Shirley simply was not interested in boys, and Mave knew it. However, Mave did not think it was natural for a girl their age to at least not be going steady with someone. Plus, she wanted to be able to double date with Shirley and her boyfriend.

Later on that night, when Gus, Jack, and Jamie went to get beer from the car, Mave asked, "Shirley, I'm beginning to think you don't like boys!"

"What? Are you accusin' me of bein' that way?"

"Well, Shirley, it jist doesn't seem like you do. Jack is a quarterback. I mean all the girls like'm, 'cept you!"

"Mave, I'm not a lesbian. Plus, Jack's an asshole," Shirley said and she walked off toward the boys, who each had a couple of beers in their hands. That night, and to Georgette's chagrin, Shirley sat close to Jamie, allowing him to shelter her from Mave's persistent demands that she find a fella.

In the tent with the soft sounds of rain hitting the canvas, Shirley wondered how many battles she would face before she was comfortable with love. The next day, the troops trekked back to camp in the rain. After cleaning herself up and resting, Shirley finally spoke to her parents.

"Hello, lemme speak to Mama."

"Oh Shirley, you are so gonna git it," retorted the little voice on the other end. The receiver dropped banging against the wall in the kitchen.

"Yep," her father answered.

"Daddy."

"Yep."

"It's me, Shirley."

"I know."

"I'm in the military."

"I know," he said and chuckled. His laughter broke the nervousness she felt. Mr. Carmichael was so glad to hear from her that any anger he may have felt dissipated. Her father said, "Baby, we could have discussed this. You didn't havta run."

"I just didn't know what else to do," Shirley said.

"We love you. We wouldn't have forced you t'marry if you weren't ready."

"And Mama—she mad?"

"Honestly, you leavin' like you did hurt. But don't you worry about it. Let me handle yer mother."

"Daddy, I—I gotta go. They don't let us talk for long. Tell everyone I said hello and Mama I love her," she said hurriedly because she could see over her cap McCalister eyeing her stopwatch.

"All right love," he said, hearing the cacophony of women in the background.

When she hung up the phone, she returned to her bunk. She had three more weeks of McCalister's yelling and hollering, and then she was locked into a four-year contract. Soon after she talked to her father, the enormity of what Shirley had done hit home, and she thought to herself, "I didn't even have t'run."

By week six, Shirley accomplished more than any girl she had ever known in Hickshaw, including Mave. She knew how to defend herself, clean a gun, survive out in the woods, and make hospital corners, in addition to her being able to see the formation of a clearly defined six-pack. Shirley was a slim girl, but between the meat and potatoes served at the chow hall and the morning and evening drills, her body resembled a well-defined machine. Going into tech school, Shirley finally began to settle into military life. She trained to be a clerk typist, and by the beginning of September, Shirley was, like other girls, making a wish list. Her wish list included Guam, Greece, Italy, Spain, Okinawa, Philippines, and Germany. Because of her field, she got her first choice, Greece. When she heard she would leave in two weeks, she called home.

"Mama. This is Shirley."

"Yep, gal."

"I'm goin' to Greece," she announced. There was silence on the other end of the line.

"Mama, you still there?"

"That's so far away. Are ya sure ya wanna go that far from home?"

"Well, it's too late if I wanna change my mind because my orders have already been set." She continued, "I have two weeks before I have to PCS, and I wanna come home first."

"PCS?" her mother asked.

"Leave," Shirley explained.

"All right. I'll put Daddy on the phone so you can speak with him."

Her mother left, and a couple of minutes later, her father picked up the receiver.

"We have a better idea. We'll come spend time with you. Can you meet us in Macon?"

"Yep."

"Then, we'll spend some time with your aunties. Haven't seen them in a while."

Her father wanted her to come home, but the whole thing with the wedding had not blown over yet, and he did not want to run the risk of bumping into anyone at church or in town, especially the Hansons.

"That'll be perfect," Shirley said.

Shirley had already known the way people in town behaved when something scandalous happened, so she was relieved not to have to face anyone. Townspeople would be cordial, but every time she turned her back on them, their whispers of admonishment were painful and loud enough to be felt, so she agreed Macon was probably a better spot to meet.

Chapter Eight — A Girlfriend

Jamie turned toward the girl with the porcelain face. She was unlike any other woman with whom he shared intimacies. He traced the outline of her body with his finger and then reached out to touch her straight black hair. He had been at one of the local bars with some of his friends from the post in Aviano and had seen her many times before he actually talked to her. She was usually in the establishment with older NCOs, guys with rank.

When she walked up beside him at the bar, and said, "Alo! Want to buy me something to drink?" Jamie looked at her, surprised by her forwardness.

"Sure. Bartender, can I have two Jagermeisters?" Jamie said.

"Not Jagermeister. I'll have a gin and club soda," she said.

The drinks came, and they began to talk. Jamie noticed how she looked at him from under her eyelids. He liked that she was so comfortable about herself with him, and her accent drove him crazy. He was so enamored by her that he ignored the looks from guys that had been probably dated her, slept with her, desired her, and coveted her. He listened solely to her. The only break in their conversation came when a particular attractive tech sergeant, TSgt Sincich, walked into the establishment. Jamie had seen them together before and made his own assumptions about their relationship.

Jamie asked more than said, "Sincich's here?" Half distracted with Jamie's chatter, she could not see whether or not Sincich came in with someone. By this time in his dating life, Jamie had become a pro at reading female body language, and he knew she would want to talk to the handsome tech sergeant.

Jamie said, "Listen, I have to run to the jon," and he excused himself, expecting her to find her way to the guy he thought she really wanted. When Jamie came back to his seat, she was still there. Jamie figured whatever business she had with Sincich was over or could wait, and so he spent the rest of the evening talking to her. When the last patron left, the two of them remained and talked to each other.

Then, at half past one in the morning, the bartender said, "We close in five, lovebirds."

Jamie asked, "Wanna go hangout?" He did not want to take her in an apartment full of guys.

"It's really late Jamie."

"Come on. It'll be fun."

The two left the bar and walked down the pebbled walkway. They eventually reached a small grassy field. Jamie held her hand. She liked holding hands. Most guys were not into holding hands.

"God," Jamie said. "It's so peaceful. You must love living here all the time."

"I haven't really lived anywhere else. I suppose I don't take advantage of it enough," she said. They both sat on the ground, and then Jamie said the words that opened her heart.

"You know, you have to be the most beautiful person I have ever met." She was beautiful, but Jamie was not talking about physical beauty. She was really nice in a different kind of way. She did not have a hidden agenda nor did she seem to have any expectations of him. Instead, she let him kiss her.

Before they could go too far into their lovemaking, she said, "Jamie, let's go inside. It's cold. Let's go to your place," and they did. When Francesca Lucia woke up the next morning, she turned to see Jamie watching her in a most tender way.

"What?" she asked Jamie.

"Nothing."

"What time is it?" she asked.

Jamie looked at the clock sitting by his bed and said, "A little after nine."

"Oh, I have to go. I am supposed to work in the restaurant," she said while rising out of the bed.

"I'm late, aah! My father's going to kill me," she said, dressing quickly. They did not have too much time to talk, but the last thing she said to him was, "Hey, I'll see you later."

He pulled her closer and asked, "When?"

"I'll call you," she said.

"You don't have my number."

Francesca did not have time for him to write it down, so she blurted out, "I'll be at Al Ristorante al Mare. It's close to the base." She then ran out the door, running into one of his roommates on the way out. The next time Jamie saw Francesca was the following weekend. He looked for her at the bar, but she did not show up. She probably was out with Sincich. Saturday turned into Sunday, and eventually, he worked up the nerve to go to the restaurant. It was quiet, and only a few diners littered the establishment. He sat at a table and waited to see if she was there. She then appeared.

"What are you doing here?" Francesca asked him, as she did not really expect for him to seek her out.

"You told me this is where I could find you," Jamie said.

She smiled and then asked, "What can I get for you to drink?"

Francesca disappeared behind the kitchen door after taking his drink order. At the bar, she watched Jamie. He was different from other Americans. He did not talk as much about all the things he could do, and he definitely emoted, their night together evidence of that. He reminded her of some of the schoolboys she dated. They only talked to her alone, as if she were a private, secret joy to be cherished. They did not want anyone to notice their interest, not because they were ashamed of her, but because they did not want to risk losing her to someone else. When she reappeared from the kitchen, he was still reading the menu.

She sat across from him and then asked, "Have you decided on anything yet?"

"It's all in Italian. Let me see," he said with a slight chuckle.

Still waiting for him to decide on what to eat, she said, "Let me make you something." Francesca left the table and came back to him with spaghetti Bolognese, a traditional Aviano dish. Over his first Italian meal, Jamie met the first woman, other than Shirley, he had ever considered dating seriously.

Dating an Italian woman was no different from than dating any other, he discovered. She could badger him and nag him like others, but she grew to love him like no other. When he told her he was out with his buddies, she knew he meant other women, but she still loved him all the same. In this same way, Jamie and Francesca became one, neither expecting too much or too little of each other.

What he loved about her was family. The first time he ate with her family, he listened as her parents told funny stories. He did not understand a lick of Italian, but when the family laughed, he laughed too, and when they listened, he listened while Francesca translated intermittently. He watched Francesca's father dote on her mother and wondered whether two people could find, and keep, love for so long without the tumult relationships could bring. By having these interactions, Jamie soon loved family, and thus Francesca. The day he asked her to marry him they fought. He did not know what else to do to show he truly loved her.

"I don't see her anymore. She's gone back to the states," he explained in earnest about his last tryst.

"You've talked to her since then, Jamie. I know you have," she said calmly after finding the small case package of remember-mes in his closet.

"Only once, and it was right after she left, Francesca. Come on, Francesca. She's not even in Italy anymore."

"Only once," Francesca repeated, and then asked, "Then what are these?" She showed him the box containing lingerie, lipstick, and picture of the comely woman. He looked at the box and brushed her hand away.

"Yeah, baby, only once," he said. "I promise." He pulled her into him, and it just was the right moment for him. His heart told him he should wait, but holding her close to him fooled him into thinking it was the love of permanence. He looked over her head.

"Are you going to be like this when we get married?" he asked.

"You want to marry me?"

"Of course, but not if you don't trust me," Jamie said. Then he married her.

Chapter Nine—Chet

As her classmates prepared themselves for the fall and higher education, Mave was no longer consumed by thoughts of an education. Instead, the first week of October she and the whole family anticipated the birth of the couple's first child. Then it happened. Mave was with her mother in their garden as her mother lectured her on her new duties as a young wife. Her mother did not hear the first scream because she was reinforcing the idea of the sacrifice women have to make for their children. However, Mave's second scream awakened her mother from her tirade. At the hospital, Chet seemed to be born in one swift motion.

"Push, gal! Push!" Mave's mother whispered in her ear as Mave labored with her first child.

"Come on, gal, push!" Her mother repeated. Mave quickly thought back to one of her classmates, Anna Marie Tuttle, telling everyone in school about her niece's birth.

"My sister said motherhood is so beautiful that once ya give birth ya forget the pain."

This pain was not any pain Mave would ever forget. She spent the last half hour between pants and breaks for ice wondering if she would ever be brave enough to have sex again, but with that last long, hard push, Chester Oliver Henriksen—Chet—came into being.

Lying in the hospital room bed, Mave experienced a multiplicity of emotions. Her kin flooded the hospital, and all day friends, cousins, grandparents, parents, uncles, and aunts came to wish her and the baby well. This day, she was also officially admitted to the grown-up club. She did not get the true grasp of what Chet's birth meant until Mrs. Hanson walked in with a pound cake.

"Thanks, Mrs. Hanson," Mave piped up from the bed.

"Oh dear, call me Louise," the young woman said casually. Then she asked, "How you feelin' hon?"

"All right, I guess. A little tired," Mave said.

The rest of the day proceeded in that way. By the end of the day, Mave learned the first names of almost all the women in the church. Even though she had been around them her whole life, her parents always made the girls address adults in the community as mister or missus. To address grown-ups by their first names was a fringe benefit of being married, at least for Mave. The highlight of the day, though, was when she saw Gus sitting in a chair in the corner cradling Chet. Watching him coo and fuss over the child temporarily erased any thoughts about her own personal desires. The longing for school left momentarily, which was probably a good thing because Chet would leave little time for studying.

In those first few weeks, Mave was consumed with around-the-clock diaper changes and feedings. In the routine of taking care of Chet, she still had a husband. Just when she put the baby down for a nap, she had to wake up to take care of Gus. Mave soon developed a schedule that allowed her to do both. When the baby slept, she slept. When the baby was awake and not crying, she took care of the chores. Sometimes when Gus was not too petered out from work, he would take over and give her an evening to herself. She and Gus were in this together forever, so she settled. One afternoon when Gus gave her a break, she went home. When she walked into the foyer, the house seemed much smaller.

"Mama," she called out to see if anyone was home, and then she set her day bag on the corner of the stair and went to the back of the house. Her mother was working outside in the vegetable garden. She stood by the screen door silently watching her mother pluck tomatoes from a vine. Her mother's matronly shape stooped over the vine, and Mave saw her mother as a woman for the first time. She wondered whether her mother had dreams independent of family and home or had her mother's life been her own a choice. In mid thought, her younger sister, Marla, interrupted her. Marla came from behind Mave, hugging her sister tightly around the waist and then running past her into the garden.

"Mama! Mama!" Marla called out from the back porch.

Her mother turned toward the commotion. "What, child?"

"Mave's back!"

Her mother turned around and saw Mave step off the porch door. Dressed in overalls, Mave pushed her hands into the pockets of the denim jeans. Her mother approached her.

"Is everything okay with the baby? You and Gus aren't fightin', are ya?"

"No, Mama. Gus let me come for a spell. I'll meet'm in church tomorra."

Her mother looked quite relieved. She turned toward Marla and said, "Go make sure your sister's bed is ready and wipe down the bathroom." After Marla left, Mave picked up the basket of tomatoes and followed her mother to the vine.

"So, how's everything?"

"I'm tired. Baby keeps me busy."

"And Gus?"

"He's fine," Mave stammered and continued. "Yeah, don't think I'll be gettin' t'school this year." Her mother paused, and then a look of concern washed over her face.

"I thought you laid that scholarship to rest when ya got married."

"I still wanna go. My scholarship is still good."

"When are ya gonna to have time, and who's gonna watch the baby?"

"I figure I could start at night, and after work, Gus could watch the baby," Mave said and then added, "He is his son too."

"Mave, no man is gonna wan t'work like a mule all day and then come home to a cryin' baby," her mother said and dropped the garden shears, turned toward her daughter, and touched her face.

"Best thing you could do is get ya heart set right on marriage. On Monday, call those people at the scholarship office and let'm know you won't be attendin'."

"But Mama."

"Lay it to rest girl. Ya gotta husband and a baby that are priorities. Lay it to rest."

The two women worked in quiet the rest of the afternoon, Mave working in internal revolt and her mother working in peace. Most mothers understand their children, but in this situation, her mother was at a loss. As a young wife, Mave's mother found it easy to adjust to the role of wife and mother. Furthermore, her mother did not understand Mave's desire for college and to be an independent woman. She had seen women in the town open businesses and have careers and knew it was possible, but Mave's mother did not understand why a woman would want to go into the world and work like a man all day long. Mave, on the other hand, saw a great benefit to being educated. As kids, a few grown-up tales of caution warned her and Shirley of not being able to support themselves, much less a family. The stories were similar in theme, with women left to care for babies when the daddy left. On top of that, Mave felt there was more to life than the family and Hickshaw.

When they finished in the garden, Mave's mother made dinner while Mave sat at the kitchen table and watched. Marla joined them, and when Daddy came home, everyone sat at the table to eat. Later that night, Marla finally got a little time with her sister. In the bunk beds they shared as kids, Mave struggled to get comfortable because the bed shrunk. Her feet kept hanging over the bed, and her head kept hitting the headboard.

"Do ya think what Shirley did was right?" Marla asked in the darkness of the room. Marla was fifteen and innocent, and the gray world had not shattered her black and white existence yet.

"Right? What do ya mean, right?"

"Leaving that boy and all."

"They weren't married, Marla. Just engaged."

"She was suppos'ta marry him."

"He didn't own her," Mave snapped, annoyed by her sister's innocent question.

"I know. I'm just sayin'," Marla said, reconsidering her words.

At the same time, Mave became aware of her tone and said, "Hey, Shirley made a good decision for herself. I really don't think she was ready t'marry."

"Have you talked to her?"

"She sent a postcard, but we haven't really talked."

The truth was Mave missed Shirley. At first, life without Shirley was hard because every day since she came into being Shirley had been a part of her life. As girls, one could not do anything without double-checking with the other. When she got married to Gus, Mave found it difficult because, even though she and Gus shared each other physically, there was an intimacy with Shirley that she and Gus would never have. Mave was learning to trust Gus, but she missed her good friend. A drowsy haze enveloped Mave, and she felt sleep overtake her.

Mave told her sister, "Don't have sex." Mave continued, "Don't have sex and don't get married until yer really sure yer ready. Make a future for yerself."

"Huh?" Marla asked, confused.

"Just don't git married," she said, and then Mave fell asleep.

The next morning everybody got up, ate breakfast, and went to church. Mave left her family and took a seat next to Gus and the baby. Meanwhile, Marla spent the entire church service mulling over her sister's warning. Mave, Gus, and Chet sat nearby in the church pews, unaware of the silent tumults marriage can sometimes bring. Mave's mother occasionally glanced toward her daughter, concerned that in marriage Mave was not settled, and this fact was plainly apparent.

Chapter Ten — A Mother-in-Law

Jamie looked into Francesca's eyes, wondering if marriage had been made a mistake. They were standing on the balcony, and the only person he could think of was Shirley. He asked Francesca to marry him because he loved her, but he did not know if he had been ready to marry. He was not actually waiting for Shirley, but when he heard she had a boyfriend, he assumed whatever they shared by the lake that day long ago when they were teenagers was lost somewhere in time, so here he was, a married man with the life that he wanted and a stable family. He kissed his wife, not feeling really romantic but settled.

"So when do you plan to tell your parents you are staying in Italy?" Francesca asked.

Her entire family lived in Italy, and the thought of living in another country so far away from everyone upset her, so he conceded on this one request from her father. Her father did not demand he remain in the country for him to marry her, but when his soon-to-be father-in-law said, "Mia figlia è speciale per me, e mi preoccupa che lei può essere perso in quella terra si chiama America," it broke his heart, and so while Jamie agreed to stay in Italy, he was not content with his decision.

He answered Francesca, "I'll tell them soon."

His mom and current man friend came over from the states for the wedding, but they left soon after to vacation on the rest of the continent. He intended to tell his mother about his plans, but he did not have the time to discuss the logistics of life with Francesca. Jamie did not see him avoiding the conversation as a problem, but Francesca did. She made it known what type of marriage she intended to have very soon after they were married. He stopped by a little flower shop outside Aviano Air Base to buy his wife some flowers. Every now and then he would make this gesture because he watched his father-in-law do it for his wife and thought it was something his wife would have missed by marrying an American. He opened the door to the little apartment the two shared outside the base. He walked into an apartment that as usual had been cleaned spotlessly. The fragrance of a home-cooked meal permeated the living space, and in usual fashion, Francesca sat on their love seat reading a magazine.

"I spoke to your mother today, Jamie," she said.

"How is she?" he asked, noticing the tension around Francesca's mouth.

"She's great. I guess," she said.

Jamie stopped talking because she ordinarily would be so talkative, but today she was withholding something. He was tired from a long day and he did not want to prolong what he knew was some minor problem she could not express. He went to the back of the apartment to shower and change. When he came back into the bedroom, she sat on the bed.

"Why didn't you tell your mother that you wouldn't be returning to America?" Francesca asked. At the time, he did not think it would be a big issue, but she was upset by this omission.

"Francesca, with getting married, visiting with relatives, and getting our lives together, I really didn't think it was of importance at the time."

"So you didn't think telling your mother that you would not be returning to your home country was important?"

"No, Francesca, it's not that big a deal for me," he said and continued, "Did you tell her when you talked to her?"

"Yeah, I blurted it out by accident and we almost argued over it," she said.

"So my mom yelled at you?"

"Yes, well, no, not really, but she's mad," Francesca said.

Jamie sat quietly for a minute or two, and then she got off the bed and stood before him. His face and upper torso were wet from the shower so she lifted his chin, avoiding the moistness of his chest.

"Hey, I don't want to fight with you," she said.

"I know. I'm sorry Francesca. I didn't mean to forget," he said.

"I know, baby. I just need you to call your mother and to tell her what is going on." He put his clothes on and then he ate the fried chicken, linguine, and grilled vegetables she made. Later on after dinner he called his mother.

"Jamie, what is this I hear about you not returnin' to the states?" his mother said before he could even ask for her.

"I was going to tell you, but with all of the business of the wedding, I just forgot."

"Jamie, you can't be seriously considerin' givin' up your citizenship."

"I'm not giving up my citizenship. I just didn't want to make Francesca leave Italy."

"What? You're in the military. She should know that you would move around."

"No, Mom, I can get a job right here on the base as a civilian when

I get out in a couple of years."

"Jamie!" she said with a raised voice, but before she could finish, he interrupted her.

Speaking over her voice, he said, "These phone calls are expensive. I don't want to spend the time arguing with you!"

Jamie could see Francesca's anxious expression across the room and he tried to keep his tone even, but talking to his mom was difficult, especially since in the last few years she had relied on him heavily. The line on other end remained quiet, and so he spoke into the receiver.

"Mom, I just called to let you know what was happening, so you would know."

"So I would know what?" She asked. Then she said, "I want to know why Francesca has influenced you to make such a rash decision."

She hit a nerve.

"My wife didn't influence me on anything, and another thing don't yell at me about her," he said.

"Well maybe if you weren't so secretive I wouldn't have to yell at you or her, she snapped. Jamie had this discussion with his mother in many different variations about many different topics, and they all ended the same.

"Okay, Mom," he said.

Maureen hung up on him.

He turned to Francesca and said, "See. I told her." He placed the phone on the wall and then walked back to the bedroom.

Chapter Eleven — Orders

Shirley and her family spent a week visiting her aunts in Macon. She intermittently thought about Mave. Shirley thought it might be better to wait to speak to her, so she could really talk to Mave the way they used to talk when they were good friends. When Shirley said her good-byes and returned to the barracks, the first thing she did was call Mave and Gus, her husband. Force of habit caused her to call the house Mave grew up in, and she briefly spoke to Mrs. Michaelson. Shirley could tell by the hesitance in the mother's voice that Mrs. Michaelson did not want to give Shirley the number. Women like Shirley were troublemakers with their unorthodox lifestyles and points of view, even though in the time that she had been gone Shirley had not really changed, except in the fact that she did not want to marry. She had no idea that Mrs. Michaelson's fears stemmed, not from any shame Shirley brought to her own family, but from the possibility that, given a chance, Mave might get ideas and flee, too.

Then Shirley explained, "Mrs. Michaelson, I'm leaving for Greece in a coupla days. I just want to say good-bye before I leave."

For Mave's mother, Shirley leaving was almost a relief. Mave's mother ultimately decided the distance would be good and gave her Mave's new number, knowing her daughter's place in the world as wife and mother would not be disturbed by Shirley's escaping her responsibilities to her fiancée. When Shirley actually called Mave, she was relieved that Mave seemed to be settled and happy.

"Mave?"

"Shirley!" Mave answered with such excitement because she had not heard her friend's voice in so long.

"I'm leavin' for Greece," Shirley announced to Mave.

"Really?"

"Yep."

"How long you stayin'?"

"My tour is for three years."

"Oh, Shirley, what are ya gonna do about the holidays?" Mave asked. Shirley had not thought about being so far away from home during those special times. She would miss the Thanksgiving feast. She would miss the Christmas Pageant and Town Soup and the all night New Years' follies at the church, in addition to the festivities and family gatherings at her own house.

"I know—but I suppose I'll find somethin', somewhere to go," Shirley said.

"Oh, Shirley, I'm gonna miss ya so much."

"Mave, I didn't call to commiserate. Tell me what's been goin' on with you. I heard you gotta baby boy now," she said.

Mave regaled Shirley with details of Chet's birth while Shirley listened intently. Mave talked about marriage, all of it. Mave felt so good because it was the first time Mave really expressed how she felt without being admonished, and consequently feeling guilty, for not wanting this life.

Before their conversation ended, Mave said, "Shirley."

"I'm listenin'."

"You did the right thing," Mave said with a slight crack in her voice, the tears in her eyes on the verge of rolling down her face. Despite Mave's chipper voice, she had been having a bad day. She and Gus were fighting about the baby and money. Her mother was of little help, as the only words of consolation that she gave to her troubled daughter was, "Man is the head of the house, so what Gus says, goes." Quite frankly, right now, Mave did not want to hear about anybody's freedom or anyone's choice.

"Oh, Mave, what's wrong? Why do ya say that?" Shirley said.

Mave could not think of a good reason that would not betray her commitment to the life she wed, and so instead she regaled Shirley with latest piece of town gossip.

Mave announced, "Duck's married."

Shirley chuckled and then said, "Well, I guess I couldn't expect him to wait around for me forever."

Both girls laughed and Mave continued, "He stood right up there in front of the whole congregation, and it was announced that again Duck Hanson would be gettin' married. Gus whispered, 'They better hope this one don't run.' I was almost fit to tears and tryin' to hold it in." When Shirley finished with Mave, she hung up feeling better about leaving for Greece.

Chapter Twelve — TDY

Coming or going?"

"Huh?" Jamie asked. He was waiting on Francesca while she got her hair styled at the airport in Venice. He was going TDY to the Philippines, and Francesca decided to get a haircut while they waited for the flight.

The young woman sitting next to Jamie asked, "Are you leaving Italy or coming?"

"Oh, I live here. Right now, I'm TDY. And yourself?" Jamie asked, not particularly interested in talking to the woman.

"Going—and I'm ready to get out of here, to be stateside."

"You didn't enjoy your tour in Aviano?"

"I mean, it was okay—I just, you know, am ready to be around my own people."

"Yeah—nothing replaces home," Jamie said.

Jamie looked at the young woman. She was pretty in a California girl kind of way. Had he not been married, he would have taken her up on her offer before the flight, but instead he remained quiet.

"My name is Noel," she said and stuck her hand out.

"Uh, I'm Jamie," he said while lightly shaking her hand.

"Where you going?"

"Philippines."

"Really? You'll enjoy yourself. It's a great place to visit, especially if you're traveling with someone. Are you with someone?" Noel asked. Before Noel could say anything else, Francesca returned to the place where she left Jamie an hour earlier.

Jamie turned, and said, "Ah, here she is. Francesca this is Noel. Noel this is my wife."

"It's nice to meet you," Francesca said, holding out her hand. Jamie then tuned out while the two women conversed. Jamie drifted off into a conversation he had with Francesca a day earlier.

"I just don't think we're ready for children," Francesca explained while dreading having this conversation about children again.

"No one is ever ready for children. My god, Francesca, you are the third of nine kids—you'd think you were used to having kids around the house," Jamie said trying to convince Francesca to conceive.

"Exactly. I've been watching over my younger siblings for what seems like forever. Plus, that's different."

"How so?"

"Well, children are a priority. I can't just skip off to play when they become too bothersome. Plus, Jamie, I want to live a little before I settle down. I don't know. I thought we'd be married a while before we had children. There's so much we should at least try to do before having a family."

"Like what, Francesca?"

"Traveling, saving money for a house."

"We can do that with children."

Francesca got up from the loveseat and walked toward the window in the apartment, leaving Jamie on the couch. This conversation was not the first they had about children, but Jamie pursued this topic in this moment because he needed to become important to someone other than his wife and his mother. He needed to have someone love him in a way that they would never want to abandon him. They both remained in the living room, each of them quiet, each of them wondering who would make the remark that would spark the argument over children this time.

Jamie said, "Francesca, why don't you want to have children with me?" Francesca turned away from the window and looked at him.

"Jamie, it's not that I don't want your children. Right now, I just don't think it's good for us."

She rejoined him on the sofa, and said, "I want to go to school, travel and see the world, Jamie. I want my children to be raised by parents who are educated, so they won't have to struggle so much. When we have money and time and we're tired of the world, we'll have more time for our children. That's all, Jamie."

Jamie never argued with his wife. For the most part, he conceded with her every demand, but lately he felt a deep need to be a husband in a very real way, which for him meant fatherhood.

"I think you're wrong. I think we'd be great parents. Your parents did it, and you turned out to be a wonderful person," Jamie said.

"My parents struggled—a lot. I spent much of my free time raising children when I should have been enjoying my life. I'm sorry. Struggle is not good." Jamie said nothing, but he got up from the loveseat and walked into the bedroom.

Later on that evening while they ate dinner in silence, Francesca said, almost pleading with him, "Please don't make me have children. I really am not ready."

Jamie remained quiet throughout dinner, and when he looked

into his wife's carryall as he packed for their trip to the Far East, he saw the diaphragm and knew in this season he would not be a father.

Chapter Thirteen — Derek

Shirley had a hard time on the flight over. She changed planes in New York and then again when she reached Madrid. In total, she spent almost thirty-six hours traveling. When she arrived, though, it was all worth it. Flying into the airport, she noticed the crystal, dark blue clearness of the Mediterranean. She had never seen such deep, blue water in her life, and the black sand was such a contrast to the white sands of the Emerald coast. She had swum in the small lakes and streams close to home, but the sea seemed so massive as if it would swallow her up.

As soon as she landed she met with her sponsor and settled into her room at the barracks. The first night after she reported to work, she slipped outside the gate to take a peek at the water outside of Souda. In her sandals, she stood as close to the shore as she could without getting wet. She was amazed at how the water trickled in between her toes and the sand.

Shirley wondered what some of the people at home would make of this scenery. Most of the boys who did serve in the military only came back with heroic tales of honor in battle. No one really talked about the landscape. She made a mental note to take pictures for Mave, as she probably would be the only person who could fully appreciate the beauty of the place.

She did not find it difficult to make friends either. Some of her closest running buddies she met at squadron picnics, where the beer flowed freely and everybody just relaxed and had a good time. At one of these picnics she met Derek. Derek was surrounded by a group of women mesmerized at his adept guitar playing.

Shirley found the women to be simple and thought to herself, "Boys playin' the guitar come a dime a dozen back where I'm from." She did not actually get a chance to talk to him until he let her cut in front of him while waiting for barbecue.

"Hey, thanks," Shirley said because she could not get over how cute he was.

"You work for the colonel," he said.

"Actually, I work under one of his secretaries but in the same building," Shirley said, hoping her shyness was not showing. "My name is Shirley."

"I know. I'm Derek."

Apart from being from the same region of the world, Shirley found she and Derek had much in common. He was from the South, Alabama specifically. He left a good life at home for adventure at the misfortune of his high school girlfriend. More importantly, like Shirley, he was searching for meaning in a life that had already been defined for him had he accepted his place in the world.

Derek worked in the same building but on a different floor. From Derek, she learned to live freely and without fear. He also had a kindness in him that she had not seen in too many of the boys she had been around, except Jamie. From Derek, she learned how to island hop. In Greece, traveling to smaller islands was cheap, and a person could see a whole lot of the Mediterranean if they desired and if they knew how to do it right.

The first time he kissed her all the fears about boys left her. With the circumstances surrounding Mave's marriage, Shirley feared men and in a way she still had not gotten over that fear before Derek. On her first trip to one of the islands, the weather had been cloudy when they arrived that Thursday night for a three-day weekend beginning the short Fourth of July holiday. That Friday, with nothing to do but watch the gray sky, Derek sat on one of the porch chairs and strummed his guitar. Shirley sat across from him reading a romantic scene in a dime store novel. Something about the tune Derek strummed took her back to the days when she, Mave, and other school friends would ditch school to swim at the pond. She placed the novel down and engaged in Derek's guitar playing. He glanced up again to see her watching him. After he finished with one tune, he leaned the guitar against the ottoman, came over, and showered kisses all over her face. At first she was taken aback and she did not know what to do, so she kissed him back. She remembered kissing Jamie and that rush of elation. With Jamie, she was learning how to kiss, so it was not really a kiss. With Derek, she felt heat. There was something different in these kisses Derek gave her, something different when a man put his hands all over a woman in lust. Never experiencing this feeling, Shirley—scared, nervous, and confused—tried to explain her lack of experience.

Derek interrupted her and said, "I know. You're a good girl. Now come on." He led her by the hand into the small bedroom where they made love. Nothing Mave talked about related to sex with Gus resembled what happened with Derek. The only caveats were that Shirley did not have a ring to legitimize the consummation of their relationship, and he was not Jamie.

Derek, sensing her hesitation, asked, "Why'd you come into the military?"

"I didn't want to get married. And you?"

"Same reason. I saw my friends marry people they didn't particularly know," Derek said.

"Same here," Shirley said thinking about Mave.

"That's why I intend to live life," he continued, "—and you should do the same."

"I'm living silly," she retorted.

"No, Shirley." Derek turned toward her. "I think I, well, I love you. But if there is something I wanna do, I'm gonna do it, and I want you to do the same. I won't get in your way—no matter how crazy the idea."

"Okay," she said, not quite understanding his meaning. "And I won't get in yours."

They passionately kissed each other slowly into the throes of more lovemaking. When Derek PCS'd to Guam the next year, she let him breeze out of her life the way he had floated in. Through the grapevine, she later learned he married a girl from the Philippines.

After Derek left, Shirley spent most of her time learning the components of her job. Between work and play, she often thought about her old life in Hickshaw. She wrote to Mave constantly, but her contact with Jamie had been sporadic. She knew he had been stationed in Italy, and it was not until well into her second year in Greece that she was able to get a good address. At that point, she pretty much traveled to every Greek island. When she wrote to him, she told him of all the amazing things she experienced. She made plans to visit other countries in Europe, but she did not take the opportunity to go to Italy until Jamie had invited her for a short visit.

The week she left for Italy was warm and humid. The trip over had been easy, and it arose in her a desire to see the rest of the continent. When she finally reached the airport, she was startled at the change in her friend. He had grown at least an inch, his hair was completely shorn, and he put on about twenty pounds of muscle. She almost walked past him when he stopped her. When he grinned, she immediately recognized him.

"Shirley? My God, look at you," Jamie said.

Stumped for words, she said, "How are you?"

Before she could ask any more questions, a slip of a girl came from behind and in an Italian accent, said, "Have you found her?"

"Yes, I'd like you to meet my friend from home, Shirley."

He then turned to Shirley and said, "This is Francesca, my wife."

Shirley was taken aback because Jamie did not say anything about a girl, much less a wife, in his letters, but that was how he was—extremely secretive.

Francesca was indeed a surprise. She looked like a porcelain doll, her features fine and defined and her skin so clear. Francesca had a heart-shaped face dotted by oval-shaped eyes that peaked out from long, straight black hair.

After they returned to Jamie and Francesca's apartment, Francesca took them to her family's restaurant where Shirley had her first authentic Italian meal of spaghetti Bolognese. She listened while Francesca's family told her old, Italian folk tales, and while she was extremely jealous, she understood why Jamie loved Francesca. Most of the week, though, she and Jamie hung out in town and he introduced her to his favorite spots.

In one store, where she purchased a souvenir for Mave, Jamie asked, "Aren't you glad you left Hickshaw?"

"At first I was anxious because I really didn't think it would be like this. But, yes, to answer your question, I am glad." She continued, "Are you thinkin' about havin' children?"

"Maybe. I don't know. I'd like to have children, but—," he hesitated. "Francesca, she's real nice, but we're so young. I still have a lot of traveling to do."

He then asked, "Why didn't you marry that fella you were dating?"

"Derek? I suppose I loved him, but neither he nor I wanted t'git married just because he was leavin'." She continued, "We both felt if we were suppose'ta be married it would have happened. Plus, he wasn't the type to settle down."

"Were you at least sad when he left?"

"Of course, but I can't hold onto someone who doesn't want to be held."

"It's simple as that, is it Shirley Carmichael?"

"For me it is."

They talked more about their plans, Jamie wanting to travel through Europe and Shirley wanting to travel to the Far East. Jamie had always considered getting his education in the military, but it never occurred to Shirley until he mentioned it.

"It's free, you know," Jamie said.

"Really? What do you plan t'study?"

"I dunno. Probably something to with agriculture or business." He continued, "You never know when you'll need it."

"What?" she asked.

"Your education," he said looking out at the Alps that surrounded Aviano.

Shirley had not thought about an education because it never once entered her mind that she could afford school until now. She put that seed in the back of her mind for planting later. The rest of her vacation with Jamie was spent touring Aviano's hotspots and enjoying the nightlife.

Chapter Fourteen — Lux

The holiday season passed, and they were well into the following December when Mave thought it a good idea to go ahead and christen Chet, as he was a little over a year old. His godparents were a close buddy of Gus's and his wife. After the christening, Mave, Gus, and the new godparents joined Mave's other family members for barbecue. While Mave, her mother, Chet's godmother, and Marla chatted on the deck, Gus, his father, and Mave's father stood over the barbecue pit watching the meat sizzle.

Mave's father looked up from the spatula and said, "Things going okay between you two?"

Gus paused a minute looking at Mave holding Chet and said, "As well as can be I guess."

Trying to reach for a concrete explanation, her father asked, "Are you and Mave settled?"

Gus did not want to go into the details of their marriage but said in general terms, "We're settling."

"What seems to be the problem, boy?" her father asked, not quite satisfied with the answer Gus had given.

After a minute of thought, Gus finally blurted out, "It's like she doesn't want to be married."

"Oh."

Mave's father expected a small problem that could be fixed with a few words of wisdom, not something so complex. Mr. Michaelson knew his daughter's aspirations for school had been dashed when the subject of marriage came up, but at the time, he, his wife, and Gus's parents could not think of another solution that would fit in with their values. Even today, standing in front of that barbecue pit enjoying the christening of his first grandson, the concept of divorce was so foreign to her father that the tidbit of advice he gave Gus was meant to hold the marriage together, not to hurt Mave. His intent was not to harm Mave, but he too had seen what happened to fatherless children—in his time and in theirs—and he was not having any of it for his family. Because her father's desire was to have his eldest daughter really commit to marriage, her father said loving words that were meant to steer Gus in the right direction.

"Let me pass this on to you," he stopped to reconsider his words. He flipped the chicken on the grill and said, "I love my daughter more'n anything in this world, and that's why I'm sayin' this t'ya." Gus listened while staring over at the women, who were busy fussing over the newly christened Chet.

Her father continued, "It would kill me to see that youngin' runnin' 'round here without no coverin'."

"I'm tryin'," Gus said with a sense of urgency.

"I know you are, son, and that's why you need to have 'nother one."

"What? We're strugglin' with this one." Gus glanced in the direction of his son's godfather, both giving each other a doubtful glance.

"Boy, listen to me when I'm talkin' to you," Mave's father said sharply and then said, "When I was young, I often heard it said among grown-ups, 'She can run with one, with more she's yours.' Give her another one. That'll settle things down for the both of you."

Without prodding, Gus would never do such a thing, especially since his first attempt at reigning in Mave ended in such horrible circumstances. He knew Mave had plans for school that she more than once let it be known she intended to carry out.

"Another baby? My Lord," Gus thought to himself but then mulled it over in his head some more.

Chapter Fifteen – Fish in Muddy Water

"The rabbit died?" Gus asked while Mave slowly pulled herself into the car seat.

"Yep," she said holding back the bitterness in her voice. "Doctor said I'm about eight weeks."

"That far along?"

"Yep," and the two of them sat quietly in the car, Gus turning the dial on the radio station and Mave staring blankly out the window. She wanted to burst into tears. Another baby would set her back at least two more years.

"What you thinkin' on?" Gus asked sensing her mood change.

"Oh, nothin'."

"Mave, we're gonna be all right," he said and touched her knee.

Mave knew they would be all right because business was picking up. They could afford this baby. The problem was Mave was not sure whether she would be all right. She let the quietness of the car motor's tune her out of what Gus was saying to her. Mave just mentally left.

When Gus dropped Mave off at home, she sat on the edge of the sofa and cried. Taking out a pen and pad, she wrote a letter to Shirley, pouring out her woes of despair. Mave could do nothing about her current situation. For her, life had dealt her its hand. She could not divorce Gus, and the other option to not have this child was a no brainer. Gus came into the room where Mave, whose tears had been all cried out, sat on the bed. He knew she had been crying, but he went to the back of the trailer, cleaned himself up, and returned to the small kitchenette table to share his evening meal with his wife.

When Mave's mother announced to the church congregation that Gus and Mave would be expecting their second child, Mave put on her expectant mother face, the same one she wore for her wedding. When Marla hosted a little shower for Mave, Mave sat grimly next to her mother until she and Gus were the focus of a toast. Sitting around the room looking at the well-wishers as if they were conspirators in this life she had become tethered to, she put on that same face of feigned joy. Both sets of parents were glad that she was finally settled.

Mave really did not understand why people did awful things people to one another in love until her second child, Alexis—Lux—was born the following December. This time the attachment was so strong and immediate that she was slightly concerned she did not feel the same about Chet. Unlike Chet, who always cried, Lux could sleep for hours without waking. She was a quiet baby. All the nurses commented that while all the other babies were screaming and crying for attention, Lux just lay silently waiting for the nurses to attend to her. Given the circumstances surrounding Lux's birth, Mave was relieved that the love she thought she would have to reach down and dig up for this child came so easily.

Gus, watching mother and daughter, found it hard to believe that his father-in-law's advice actually worked. He was anxious as well because it was Christmas time, and his mother and father would be staying to help Mave with the baby for a couple of days, which would mean more stress. Gus just wanted his family to settle down and grow. He was making good money, great money actually, and he could begin to think about moving his family to a larger domicile.

"Hey," he said quietly to Mave one day as he watched her with his child.

Mave still fussing with the baby said, "What?"

"Pa says that business looks like it's gonna to be on the upturn fer a while with industry and such comin' to town."

"Yeah," Mave said while playing with Lux.

"Think we oughta think about investin' in a home?"

"You think we're ready for that?"

"We've got a lot saved, some left over from the weddin' and with the sale of the trailer. Plus, we're gonna need the room."

Mave momentarily considered whether she would have more kids and then said, "Well, Gus, you do what's best."

"I mean we're not movin' right now. Let's think on it."

"All right," Mave said and, preoccupied with the baby, she began to hum a lullaby to the child.

This time around, Mave thought, she was going to enjoy motherhood. All of the little milestones that she disengaged with Chet, so distracted by her own miseries, she would engage in with Lux. Mave figured she had to be in this place, so she just decided to make the best of it. Even with trying to make the best of it, she found that being a mother had not been all her mother and other women of her mother's age and experience said it would be. On several occasions, she broached the subject with Gus, but found herself on the losing end of a battle that Gus already won before it started.

"I wanna go to school," Mave demanded while standing in front of the kitchen window after cleaning the dishes.

"Oh, God, Mave, for chrissakes, not this again," Gus said,

completely frustrated with having this conversation.

"What, Gus? You don't wanna hear what?"

"I'm tired of hearin' this shit. We're married, and I just don't see how you goin' to school is gonna make life better for us, for you."

"Gus, I need to do this. I'm goin' crazy sittin' in this house all day with these children."

"They're our children," Gus said, pleading with her.

"Gus, look, I thought we decided when the money was right and we could afford it, I'd start school," she said.

"What do you think a degree is gonna do for you? I mean ya gotta husband, beautiful children, and soon ya'll have a house. You got mon—"

"Gus, no. I just wanted to do somethin' on my own," Mave interrupted. Before he could answer, Lux's cries interrupted the conversation. Mave did not move for a minute.

Gus asked, "Mave, are ya gonna stand here and argue with me or are ya gonna go tend to my child?"

Mave threw the hand towel on the table, and then she walked toward the back of the trailer. Mave picked up Lux, who at this point was Mave's only comfort, and she walked back into the small kitchen, where Gus was sitting at the little dinette eating a chicken salad sandwich. The fixings were still on the counter and it annoyed Mave, as she had just washed the dishes.

"Gus, are you gonna put this mayonnaise away? I just cleaned," Mave asked and said in a commanding way. Gus did not say anything at first because he knew she was not angry about the mayonnaise.

"Gus!" Mave said, holding the baby on her hip.

"What, Mave? I'm on my lunch hour. I'll clean it up before I go."

"That mayo is gonna go bad settin' on that counter." He put his sandwich down on the plate and put the mayo away, and then he returned to his original spot. He began to eat.

"Gus, you forgot to wash your knife."

Gus looked at her, and then picked up his sandwich. He stood up from the table and began to walk in the direction of the door.

"Where are you goin'?" she asked.

"Mave, I have an hour for lunch, and I don't intend to spend it here arguin' with you about mayonnaise," he said. Gus took his sandwich and glass of iced tea and walked out of the door. Lux began to fret, and so Mave cradled the small child, pulling her close to her. Mave sat on the loveseat and comforted the child by cooing and looking into her green eyes.

"Lux would never have this life," Mave thought to herself.

For Lux, Mave envisioned a life more satisfying than loving a husband and children. Yes, Lux would graduate at the top of her class in high school, but this would be the point at which the lives of the mother and daughter would diverge. See, Lux would be smart enough, if she did play around with boys, to protect herself. Lux would have a few high school boyfriends, but afterward she would head straight to college.

Mave did not care what university Lux attended. Mave just knew Lux was headed for some great college where Lux would have the keys to success handed her. Lux would graduate, again with high honors, with a degree in communications, a degree that would prepare her for a life of adventure. Lux would get her feet wet doing small assignments locally, and then she would get picked up by one of the big stations.

Eventually, in her late thirties, she would travel to other countries covering international stories, eventually landing a spot as an anchor on one of the big three. She would do something beyond Hickshaw.

Whether she got married or not was inconsequential to Mave. For right now, Lux rested in Mave's arms, a bundle of joy in which all of Mave's hopes and dreams laid. Mave cradled the baby for a little while longer, and then she put Chet down and his sister down for a nap. She would get supper started around by 4:00 p.m., and by 5:30 p.m., Gus would walk through the door, and they would be a family again.

With one baby, managing a home in addition to housework was difficult to handle. With two, housework became less of a priority. The house stayed tidy, but the afternoons where she had extra time to clean every crevice in the trailer were gone. She felt lucky enough if she got Gus's food on the table before he arrived home for lunch and dinner. She thought they had enough room, but she recognized in the near future she would need to move.

"Gus, honey, should we start lookin' for a home?"

"You beginnin' to see my point?" he asked.

"I just didn't think we're gonna need the extra room so soon," she said.

"I know the Smith place is up for sale, and he's tryin' to sell quickly."

"Do we have enough to put down and for furniture? I really don't wanna put a lot down on time," she said.

"We can put $1,000 down and the remainder we use to furnish the house."

"I don't think we should just look at the Smith house. Let's look around. They're building a new development closer to Macon. Maybe we'll find somethin' there," Mave suggested, hoping he would agree.

"Okay. Let me talk to my dad. Maybe he can help us find a good person."

Exhausted, Mave put the children to bed, ate a little something, and snuggled in next to Gus on the sofa. Perched next to him on the couch, they watched Hawaii-50. She briefly thought about Shirley, being so alone and so far away from home, and snuggled even closer to her husband. It was during times like this one that she felt she made a great decision to be with Gus.

The next morning, during her trip to the furniture store, she was browsing in one of the outlets just outside of Macon when she ran into Mrs. Hodsteter, one of her favorite teachers who wrote Mave a recommendation for the scholarship to Hickshaw Community College. Mave saw the look of admonition on her teacher's face, as Mrs. Hodsteter did a cursory glance at the two babies sitting in the stroller Mave pushed.

"Mave—Mave Michaelson, is that you?" Mave looked up at her teacher, surprised. She tried to push the stroller into the aisle so as not to obstruct anyone's path.

Mave said, "Hi, Mrs. Hodsteter."

The older woman peered into the buggy at the babies and said, "How are you?"

"I'm fine. Got married year before last to Gus. We have two children now," Mave blurted out.

"Well good for you. My two are off at college." Her teacher said in reflection, "But I see them every now and then."

Mave explained, "I put off my plans for school until later."

"You have plenty of time," her teacher said, sensing Mave's embarrassment.

Mrs. Hodsteter closed the conversation with, "If you ever need me to write another letter, don't hesitate to ask."

With two kids, both of them knew Mave would wait a while before she would have the chance to even think about school. Knowing this fact, Mave changed the subject to goals she was able to accomplish since high school.

"Gus and I are buyin' a house," she said, which was not exactly the truth, but she did not want her teacher to think this time spent out of school was in vain.

"That's wonderful," Mrs. Hodsteter chuckled and continued, "Well, how's Shirley?"

"She left for the military right before school let out."

"Oh, what's a girl gonna do in a man's war?"

"Lots. She's a clerk. She's in Greece right now."

"You are full of surprises today, Mave Michaelson, aren't you?" Mave hadn't heard her maiden name in quite a while. They both laughed, finished up the conversation, and then said their good-byes. As the older teacher headed in the direction of the parking lot, Gus approached Mave.

"Was that Mrs. Hodsteter you were talkin' to?" Gus asked.

"Yeah, she was surprised about Shirley." Mave continued, "I guess she figured Shirley the marryin' type as well."

Gus chuckled. Mave shot him a warning look and he smiled. He hugged Mave and she pushed him away. She thought about the scholarship as she watched Mrs. Hodsteter head to her car in the lot. Mave did not really feel badly about the scholarship or even about bumping into her old teacher, except every time she got settled in her mind about her children and her marriage, there would be something to throw her out of that peace. When she and Gus returned, they had no sooner walked into the trailer when the phone rang.

"Mave! It's Shirley."

"Hey! How are you?"

"I got yer letter," she said, this letter a brighter picture than those

Mave sent previously.

Shirley thought it best to call because, although Mave's letter sounded brighter, Shirley had been worried. The first letter she received from Mave months before was heart wrenching, so much to the point of making Shirley feel as though she abandoned her friend in a selfish attempt to avoid her own marital duty. The lines in the letter that reverberated were, "I've been in a place I don't want to be for so long," and, "I'm stuck." The one time Shirley left a message with Gus, she knew either he never gave it to her or sometime had passed before she had received the message.

"I'm fine. How's everything with you?" Mave said.

"Still missin' Derek, but everything's okay."

"Did you tell him how you felt before he left?"

"Yeah."

"And he still left?"

"Mave, our relationship wasn't like that."

"But you slept with him," Mave said, surprised at the accusatory tone of her own voice.

"Yeah."

"Shirley, it's gonna to be all right. Just don't make that mistake again," Mave cautioned.

"Mave, it wasn't a mistake. We had an understandin'."

"What? Shirley, tell me yer not gonna be like that," Mave said.

"Like what?"

There was silence on the phone for about a minute, and then Mave said, "Loosy goosey. You know you've never been that type of girl. Hell, we used to gossip about them. I just don't want you to become that person."

Shirley did not say anything, and then she said, "He was my first, Mave, not my thirtieth."

"Still, Shirley, do you ever intend t'git married?" In the military, no one talked about what they did, but it was not the end of the world to not be a virgin and unmarried.

Shirley retorted, "Yes, Mave." Then she added, "How's it different from what you and Gus done?"

"Shirley, come on now, we're married."

"But you weren't, and for at least five or six months," Shirley said and then regretted those words. In a more conciliatory tone, Shirley said, "Mave, I called because I got yer last coupla letters. I've been tryin' to reach you, but this is the first time I been able t'talk to you. I'm callin' because I wanna make sure yer alright."

Mave reflected on the letters she sent and said, "Oh, Shirley you know me. I'm fine. As a matter a fact, Gus and I are gettin' ready to purchase a home."

"That's wonderful," Shirley said, unsure whether the calm in Mave's voice was temporary or permanent.

"Where do you plan on movin'?"

"Oh, we're still lookin'," Mave said. They were quiet for a minute.

"How's the baby?" Shirley asked and then interrupted her own self, "I sent you guys somethin'. I hope you like it."

"She's fine. You know she was born two days before Christmas."

"Yeah, that's what Mama said."

Mave, trying to make up for her earlier comment, added, "Shirley, I'm not tryin' to judge you."

"I know."

Mave added, "You play 'round like that, and you can find yerself in a real predicament."

"I know. I know, Mave."

They sat quietly for a couple of minutes when Mave said, "I better go. We just got back from town, and Gus is eyein' me to cook dinner."

The two friends hung up with each other, Shirley recognizing the chasm developing between her and her closest friend. For Mave, life was simple. There were not any blurred lines. Shirley, on the other hand, could not fit herself into that black and white world anymore. She tried to push the fears aside, but she knew that the widening chasm had little to do with the distance. Something in Shirley had changed.

Chapter Sixteen — Maureen

Jamie sat across from Francesca in their dining room. The room was small, but big enough for Francesca to fit a dining room table. Jamie picked at his vegetables, hoping that Francesca would drop her current line of questioning.

"Is there something wrong with the vegetables?" she asked.

"No, why do you ask?" Jamie answered, slightly distracted.

"You are just pushing the food around on your plate," she said. "Well, anyway, I want you to take me to your home."

Jamie panned the cramped dining space and then placed his fork on the table and crossed his arms.

"Why?" he asked.

Francesca was surprised by the question but also disturbed by his response.

"What are you afraid of? Come on, Jamie, we've been married over two years. Don't you think it's time we visit your mother?"

"You met my mother at the wedding."

"Briefly. I didn't get a chance to know her. Come on, you can take me to Disney and to see your father in South Florida."

Jamie mulled it over in his head, and then said, "Okay, we'll go in January. I'll take a little leave."

Jamie, at dinner, was not concerned, but later that evening while sleeping, he became very afraid that Francesca would come to know who he had been in Hickshaw. Francesca would be the only girl he would bring home beside Shirley, and when he brought Shirley home, it was because she forced him.

"Why don't we study at your house today?" Shirley asked one day as they both discussed where they should study. "It'll be a whole lot quieter than at mine."

The both of them needed a quiet place while Shirley explained the complexity of the Pythagorean Theorem to Jamie. Not quite comfortable with the idea, Jamie realized Shirley had been right because Shirley's little brothers were known to kick up a ruckus after school. There would be no silence in the Carmichael home until dinner. Jamie's house might be better. He needed to understand the concept to pass the test and the class. The worse part of taking Shirley to his home is that he did not know what he would find at home that day. When they both reached the house, Jamie already knew his mother had company because Mr. O'Connell's gold Ford sat in the gravel driveway.

"Wait here," Jamie said. He walked into the house to find his mother and her current beau on the couch in an intimate embrace.

"Jamie," his mother said in a voice an octave higher than her speaking voice, "What are ya doin' home?"

"It's almost three," he said and then continued, "Anyway, me and Shirley need to study. We're gonna be in my room." Jamie went back out to the porch where Shirley sat in his mother's rocking chair.

"Come on," he said and led her by the hand into his room.

"Isn't that Mr. O'Connell," Shirley asked, and the look on Jamie's face spoke a thousand words.

"Oh Jamie. I'm sorry."

"Please don't say anything to anyone."

"I promise. I won't," she said.

Shirley placed her books on the bed, and said, "Where should we start?"

In that moment with Shirley, Jamie had been able to tell her the one thing, the most important thing, about his life that made Hickshaw so painful for him. He was not so sure about Francesca understanding that person, as Francesca's mother was a conventional woman totally devoted to her children and family. Jamie did not know how to explain his mother and his upbringing.

Chapter Seventeen — A Homecoming

Shirley tried her best to keep in contact with her family and friends, but it was difficult. She had started school, and the many evenings that were once free became consumed with homework and classes. She was two courses short of her associate's degree when she got her orders for Okinawa. Before she left Greece, she went home for a month to see everyone from Hickshaw. She would not have bothered to visit, but the last Christmas she spent in Greece, she missed her family so much it threw her into a mild depression.

Shirley talked to her parents, and they were especially glad this Christmas holiday would be spent with their daughter. Mave also was happy to spend some time with her old friend. Landing in Atlanta, Shirley boarded the Trailways bus headed to Macon. Because Shirley's family was tied up with church, Mave and Gus offered to pick her up from the bus depot in Macon.

When the friends laid eyes on each other, the change in each other had been marked. Mave stubbornly held onto an extra ten pounds that hung on her petite frame even though she spent the previous three months dieting. A plain blue T-shirt and jeans were complemented by a set of curls pulled back into a ponytail. Shirley, still firm and fit, slipped into a pair of flared denim jeans with cowboy boots to match. She wore a leather jacket and a knit halter top. Her long hair hung loosely under a suede cowboy hat. Her skin glowed as if she had just returned from a beach getaway. Gus saw her first.

"Hey, isn't that Shirley?"

"Shirley! Shirley!" They both called out. Shirley looked up, and there the two of them stood.

"Come here. Let me look at ya," Mave said. "You are a sight for sore eyes." She turned to Gus and said, "Look what the military sent us."

Gus just gawked, amazed at the transformation.

On the ride home, Shirley listened to Mave talk mostly about the way the town changed in the two and half years she had been gone.

"Well, Mr. Peterson sold the store, and they built a Kmart. I guess with the new industry they felt it would attract enough customers to support the store."

"Oh, really? They're leavin' the candy store?" Shirley asked.

"No, that went right along with it."

"You're kidding me," Shirley said with slight nostalgia and regret.

As they approached the town limits, Mave continued, "Yeah, me and Gus are thinkin' about movin' to one of the new developments closer t'Macon."

Gus added, "By the time they finish, everybody's sayin' this ole' hole in the wall might be a suburb of Macon. At least that's what the developers keep sayin'."

When they passed the place where Peterson's General Store and Ice Creamery had been, all that was left was gravel and what had been a small parking lot.

"Why did Peterson sell?"

"For the same reason as the others, big economy," Gus explained.

"What?"

"My dad said they expect this place to see big economy. When industry comes, so does all sorts of opportunities for the community," Gus explained.

"I suppose Peterson made a good decision," Shirley said.

Mave turned to Gus and watched him explain the intricate details of town business to Shirley. She was so proud of the life they had built together. Lately, Gus and Mave had been asked to host get-togethers at the chamber of commerce, which meant they were moving up in the social trajectory of Hickshaw society. Mave was happily surprised that Gus had some get-up-and-go to him.

Gus finished explaining, "Take the opportunity to sell, hold onto his money, and then when the time is right, reinvest."

"Oh," Shirley said still stuck on the fact that a town landmark had been erased. They sat quietly for a minute and then Shirley asked,

"Has Jamie been home yet?"

"I think he passed through here a while back. He didn't spend too much time visiting, though," Gus said and then added, "Yeah, he and that girl he brought with him to church, I guess they had enough of us," he finished looking in the rear view mirror to see Shirley's reaction.

"Long black hair, real pretty, Italian accent?" she asked.

"Yep. They got married in Italy a couple years ago. Apparently, it was a big shindig. His mom's still talkin' about it," Gus said.

"Oh, that's Francesca," she returned, staring right back Gus.

"Well, he introduced her to us as Fran," Gus said.

"Oh, Gus, it's all the same," Mave said.

The three continued to talk, each having their own separate thoughts about Jamie. Jamie hung out with them, but even so, they never felt he was a part of their social group. The closest person to him was probably Shirley, but even she was kept from the most secret parts of his life. Gus and Mave shrugged Jamie's secrecy off while Shirley was always disappointed that Jamie did not feel close enough to her to share his world. Nevertheless, she placed his marriage and Francesca to the back of her mind. When they reached the Carmichael house, Shirley reached back into the cab of the truck and grabbed the few things she bought to stay with her folks.

"I'll probably see you in church Sunday. My parents are gonna wanna spend some time with me," Shirley said before closing the truck door.

"All right. Catch up with you later," Mave said.

In church Sunday, she sat next to Mave, Gus, and the children. Afterward, they were to spend a little time at Patsy's. She sat through the service listening to the preacher tell the story of Abraham and Lot for the millionth time, and just halfway through her second yawn, she understood Lot's dilemma. Shirley was annoyed that while the congregation listened to this story so many times, they behaved as though it was the first telling. In the same place, the congregation gave their amens and hallelujahs as in previous retellings, clapping and shouting in the most appropriate places.

Shirley looked around the church-filled pews at the rapt attention of the congregation. She saw Duck and his new wife up front and center. Her own parents and siblings were in the pews behind them. Mave's parents sat next to hers and Gus's sat right in front of Shirley, Mave, Gus, and the children. Sitting in the middle of the congregation, Shirley became keenly aware of the way people change but stay the same. Everyone in Hickshaw aged. They had, but it seemed like the two and half years that had passed tripled, and everyone was ten years older but the same.

"Don't be afraid to come home," were the words Mave yelled in the darkness of that May night almost three years ago, and they reverberated in her head as she listened to the congregation say a collective "Amen" when the pastor stopped preaching. After church, she watched everybody engage with each other. She talked to some people, but she soon realized that her once-defined place in this community was becoming muddied by her own actions. Leaving her childhood home, to some, had been an act of rebellion, so she had been silently pushed to the margins of Hickshaw community life. Shirley did not know exactly who took her place until just before she and Mave went to lunch.

Shirley and Mave stood in the parking lot waiting on Gus to drop the kids off with his parents when Jolene approached the three of them and said, "Hey, Mave. I just wanted to talk to you before we all got out of here today."

"Hey, Jolene." Mave said. Feeling kind of awkward with Shirley standing there, Mave said, "Let me introduce you to Shirley."

Jolene was a much different picture than Shirley had imagined. Shirley expected someone with a bun at the back of her head who wore long dresses and baked pies for every occasion, but what stood before her was a woman used to hard work. Jolene wore the requisite church clothing, but she had a worn look. Her mousy brown hair was held together by ribbon and the cowboy boots she paired with her country frock spoke of a woman who worked even while she was at rest.

A knowing glance passed between Mave and Jolene, and Shirley felt the full sting of the silent message that passed between the two women. Previous to this moment in their histories, Mave always referred to Shirley as her best friend. This time was the first that Shirley had been given a different, lesser designation in friendship. Shirley and Mave had always been loyal to each other in their in youth, but time and distance placed a chasm between the two of them.

Shirley said, "Hello, I'm Shirley Carmichael."

"Well, it's nice to meet you," she said cordially, but all three women knew too well the untold narrative that hung like a thick sheet of smoke in the air.

Jolene continued, "I jist want to make sure that you and Gus would be join'n us this coming Saturday for the Young Businessman's Potluck over at the chamber."

Mave said, "We'll be there. I'm glad you stopped by. I'm not sure I'd've seen you this week to tell you, but yes, Gus mentioned somethin' 'bout it."

Jolene reached out to kiss Mave on the cheek and said, "We'll see ya' then."

When Jolene was out of earshot, Shirley asked, "You two friends?"

"It's business,"Mave said.

"She seems nice."

"Actually, she's real nice," Mave said. Both of them remained quiet for a moment, each secretly going over their own thoughts about what just transpired.

Then Shirley said, "Let's go to Patsy's. Haven't been there in a while."

Both of the women got into Mave's truck to go to the diner. While other businesses decided to leave Hickshaw, Patsy's still remained a staple in town. The owner, Patsy Jones, was preparing to feed some of the industry they predicted would give Hickshaw a makeover. Patsy had new tables and countertops installed, and she arranged to have someone work on the exterior of the place as well. They sat at a booth facing the street. Mave ordered the chicken fried steak entrée, and Shirley ordered smothered pork chops. They spoke intermittently between bites, but not until they shared a banana split did illusions of their friendship become removed.

"So, you're goin' to Japan?" Mave asked.

"Not really. It's Okinawa, an island off the mainland."

"Oh, so are you excited?"

"Yeah, I'm hopin' I can go visit some of the countries in that region."

"Really? Won't that be expensive?"

"We can take a hop."

"A hop?"

"Get a free ride on a plane if it happens to be goin' in the same direction."

"Oh," Mave said. They both sat quietly each slurping on a corner of a banana split.

Then Shirley said, "I'm in school."

"What?" Mave asked surprised.

"Yeah, I'm in school. I'll finish my associate's degree by the end of this year," and then she added, "If I start school as soon as I get to my station."

A piece of cherry that Mave chewed on got stuck and then slid to the back of her throat. Mave swallowed hard.

"How you gonna pay for school? Isn't it expensive?"

"It's free. The military pays for it. Jamie told me about it."

"Oh," Mave said.

By this time, a lump had formed in Mave's throat, and the lump moved into her stomach, as if her throat closed and she inhaled a brick, which was taking her forever to swallow. Mave suddenly felt uncomfortable with herself because usually she was happy when someone had good news. However, all she felt was not so much envy of Shirley but momentary regret for herself.

She just reached her hand out to Shirley and said, "Good for you, sweetheart."

The girls finished up at the diner and stopped by Mave's parents' house to drop off some clay pots Shirley picked up in Greece for Mave's mother. Mave was quiet most of the visit as she listened to Shirley chatter about the use of the pots and their origins. While she put the idea of school away, Mave knew deep down she had not silenced that little voice in her spirit that constantly nagged her about her own education.

When Mave dropped her friend off at home, the last thing she said to Shirley before Shirley left was, "Good luck to you, Shirley Carmichael." Mave said these words knowing it would be a while before she set eyes on Shirley again.

Chapter Eighteen — Maureen

Jamie and Francesca sat outside in the rental car for a moment before going into his childhood home.

"Okay, let me just tell you. She's a little bit different but—" Jamie said but did not finish his sentence.

"Jamie, can we just go in? I know your mother is a little different. I've talked to her on the phone and met her at the wedding."

"I know, but I don't want you to expect—"

"Jamie, we've been traveling all day. I just want to go inside and wash up."

Jamie opened up the car door and walked back to the trunk to get the bags. By this time, Francesca was on the porch waiting for him. Jamie knocked on the door, but there was no answer. He checked to see if the door was open. He walked into the living room, which by now had been converted into a hangout for hippies. His mom always current in living room décor decorated the home with staple items from the late sixties. The beads that hung in the doorway swayed back and forth making a loud noise.

"Wait here a minute," Jamie said and walked down the hallway. Right before he could open the door, his mom came down the hall.

"Jamie, hey, sweetie—how you doin'?" He turned to see her. He hugged his mother and looked behind her.

"Is Johansson here?"

"No. So, did you bring her?"

"Yeah, she's outside," he said leading the way back into the living room.

Maureen said to Francesca, "Hi, it's gonna be nice to spend some time with you. We didn't really get to talk at the wedding."

Francesca took in Jamie's mom. Her tousled hair and the cigarette with its burning ashes falling haphazardly on the linoleum floor of the tiny kitchen left Francesca with an understanding as to why Jamie did not really talk about his family, especially his mom. The silk kimono wrap Jamie bought for his mother while on TDY hung loosely from his mother's body. The robe slipped from its normal position, showing Francesca a glimpse of his mother's slightly exposed breasts. Catching Francesca's glance before she said anything, the older woman quickly covered herself. The two women talked while Jamie was in the back making sure his room was presentable. Then his mother called into the back bedroom where Jamie was still tidying the space.

"Jamie, I didn't have time to cook, so we're gonna havta go to Hojo."

"Okay, that's fine."

His mother walked to the back of the house and said to Jamie, "She's real gorgeous without the make-up. I don't know what she sees in you."

He smiled. "Play nice."

"Oh, I'm just kiddin'," His mother said and then asked, "So, what's the plan?"

"She wants to go to Disney World."

"How cute."

"Jamie? Jamie?" Francesca said, interrupting the pair's conversation. Then she asked, "Oh, this is your room?"

Francesca stepped into the dark blue space. The walls were littered with posters from various concerts Jamie attended as a teenager. Elvis Presley, Chuck Berry, and Jerry Lewis all hung in different places on the wall. Jamie's fishing rod and hooks were in the corner of his room, and on the small bureau sat old baseball cards. Jamie looked around the room also noticing how, even though it had changed, the room also remained the same. He outgrew the room, and standing in the middle of it in his leather jacket and jeans, he felt tall in such a small space. Francesca interrupted his thoughts again.

"Where can I wash up, Jamie?" This traveling—it takes a lot out of me."

"Oh, hon, over here. I can show you," his mom said.

As the two walked over to the bathroom down the hall, Jamie remained in the room and reminisced. He walked over to his stack of Marvel comics, and he looked for a Marvel comic given to him by his first girlfriend. He thumbed through it, and then he placed it back in the stack. As he finished, Francesca walked in right behind his mother.

His mother then turned to the two of them and said, "Give me a couple of minutes, and I'll be ready." His mother left the two of them in the room. Francesca sat on the bed and patted the mattress.

"Come sit," she said. Jamie sat down next to her.

"Well, what do you think?" he asked.

"What do you mean what do I think, Jamie?"

"Come on, Francesca," he said waiting a moment.

"Your mom is nice, Jamie."

"I know it's not what you're used to."

"Oh, Jamie what's that supposed to mean?" Before he could explain, his mom came into the room.

"How's this?" She asked while modeling a denim wrap around skirt and a halter top.

"You look great, Mom," Jamie said.

"Come on, let's go before it gets too crowded."

They had all piled into the car when the thought occurred to Jamie to ask his mother if Johansson would be joining them. At this point in the visit, things were running smoothly and Jamie did not want to start an argument, so he waited for an opportune time.

When his mother brought Johansson up, Jamie asked, "Will he be coming to dinner?"

"Maybe. You know he's in the middle of this divorce. His wife can be such a bitch about everything. I mean, my God. This man hasn't touched her in over five years. Did she think he's gonna wanna stay married? Hell, sex is the best part of the marriage. She should just let go—" his mother said.

Before she could finish, Jamie interrupted and asked, "Well, how's everything going with the girls?"

Dinner with his mother and his wife went by this tempo. He would listen to the two of them talk, and when his mother began to say something too dysfunctional, he would interrupt with a question that took his mother in another direction. When the food came, the three of them ate quietly, and then Johansson arrived and slid into the chair next to Maureen.

"Sorry I'm late. Jane has this way of makin' a simple act theater, for chrissakes," Johansson said about his wife. Jamie's mother ignored the comment and introduced her boyfriend to her daughter-in-law. Assessing Johansson's attire, she noticed nothing seemed to be out of place, except that his tie was missing.

"Where's your tie?" Jamie's mother asked. Johansson looked down at his chest.

"Shit. I must've forgotten to put one on tryin' to get out of that house," Johansson answered, knowing the implication behind the question his mother asked. His mother, used to the artful way men dodged questions about their wives or girlfriends, chose her words carefully to avoid embarrassing her son.

"You didn't get dressed at the apartment?" Jamie's mother asked. At this point, Jamie looked at his mom, almost pleading with her not to continue that line of questioning.

His mother looked at Francesca and asked, "How's your steak, sweetie?"

"It's good. I've never eaten meat grilled this way. Tasty," Francesca said taking another bite. Johansson remained quiet, glad that the topic of conversation had shifted from his tie to Francesca's steak. Maureen ignored Johansson for the rest of the meal.

Then his mother turned to Johansson and said, "You're gonna havta get somethin' to go." After dinner, the three stood in the parking lot waiting for Johansson to get his food.

"I'm gonna ride home with Billy," his mother said to both Francesca and Jamie.

When Johansson returned to the three of them, Jamie and Francesca climbed into the vehicle, and Jamie drove her around Hickshaw showing her some of his old hangouts.

After about two hours of driving around town, Francesca said, quite irritated, "I want to go back to the house, Jamie." He did not say anything at first.

"Jamie, take me back to the house."

"Okay, I heard you the first time. You don't have to snap at me."

"I just don't understand you. This whole time, I don't get what you are afraid of."

"What do you mean?"

"All through dinner, you're cutting your mother off, interrupting her, and now this two-hour adventure. You were rude, Jamie. What? You don't want me to see your mother fighting with her boyfriend who might be still sleeping with his wife?"

"Stop!"

"What is it, Jamie?"

"Stop it!"

"It's like you are trying to hide from me that your mom is—"

"Shut the fuck up! Just shut up, Francesca!" he yelled and slammed on the breaks.

"Jamie, stop!" she said, putting her hands on the dashboard. They both sat in the car not saying a word to each other, with only the sound of crickets and the birds interrupting the quiet argument the two were having.

Jamie looked at Francesca in profile and said, "Not everyone is going to have a perfect family."

"I never accused you of not having a perfect family. I accused you of hiding it from me."

"Why would you marry me knowing this about my family?"

"Oh, Jamie, I loved you. I love you. I just didn't understand why your mother's private life was such a big secret, such a big deal."

"It only mattered because I wanted you to like her."

"And I do," Francesca said and turned to kiss him. "Come let's go back. I'm tired and I need to get some rest."

Jamie rode with Francesca mostly in silence with one hand on the wheel and the other holding Francesca's hand. When the two arrived at his mom's house, they met his mother, who at this point in the evening sat on the porch.

"You two in for the night?" his mother asked.

"Yeah, Jamie wants to visit some friends in Macon, so I need to get some sleep," Francesca said, and then she walked back to the bathroom where she got ready for bed. Jamie sat on the edge of the stoop, sweeping his leather jacket from under his bottom and pulling out a cigarette. He lit up the cigarette and then pulled out another one, lighting it for his mother. They both took a long drag off the cigarettes and blew the smoke out into the air.

Silence filled the air, and Jamie's mom said, "Have you heard from that colored gal you used to see in high school?"

"I never really saw her but at school and you stopped that." He continued, "Why?"

"What was her name?" his mother asked.

"Carlotta Johnson."

Carlotta was the first colored girl he kissed. He was in the tenth grade and she in the ninth. He did not remember how they ended up together, but she was an avid comic book collector too. She gave him her favorite comic, and they became close friends. Soon after, he kissed her and she kissed him back. The first time he was with her was the last. His mother returned from a movie early after fighting with one of her boyfriends and gave the young woman the once over. Maureen told Jamie to stop seeing her and so he did.

"You heard from her?" his mother asked.

"No, what's she up to?"

"She works over at the library," his mother said.

"How's she doin'?"

"Went to college."

"Really?"

"Yeah."

His mother's next words surprised him.

"Had I had any sense I would have let you date her."

Jamie looked at his mother, not knowing how to interpret her last comment.

"I thought you were against miscegenation."

"Miscge-what?"

"Race mixing."

"I dunno. That's what everybody tells you is right, but I'm not so sure. At this stage in the game, for me, love knows no color."

"He's still with his wife, isn't he?" Jamie asked, knowing this conversation was not really about race relations in Hickshaw.

"Yep," his mother answered meekly with a hint of tiredness in her voice, and then she put out the cigarette and walked into the house. Jamie soon followed his mother into the house and got himself ready for bed. Then he lay beside Francesca, waiting for something in his heart to change, to open up, to tell him it was safe for him to love like most do, without the pain.

Jamie and Francesca visited his mom for three days, went to Disney, and then spent the rest of their vacation in Florida, where he formally introduced her to his dad and his new family, who had relocated to Central Florida.

Chapter Nineteen – Friends

Mave dreaded going over to the Hanson place. Jolene and Duck were young, rich, and happily married—everything she and Gus were not. She hated driving the long, winding road into the Hanson estate, as it reminded her of a plantation that still was in the midst of its glory days. As she traveled the dirt road that was a part of the plantation, Mave stared out at the plush green pasture on both the left and the right side of the road.

The first edifice she saw was on Papa's Patch. Papa's Patch was named after the lot of land Duck's father used to create his fortune. With no more than twenty acres, Papa Hanson was able to turn his small plot into a viable self-operating crop business. Mave could not help but feel a little jealous of Jolene and Duck. When the two were married a few months after Gus and Mave, Duck's parents set them up with not only a large, four bedroom ranch-style home, but his father, with his business connections, was able to secure for his boy a seat on the board at the town's chamber of commerce, accomplishments that would take Gus and Mave almost ten years to do on their own. As she walked up the porch steps, Mave could not help but wonder how much more jealous of Shirley she would have been had Shirley married Duck instead of Jolene.

Mave rang the doorbell and waited a couple of minutes. When no one came to the door, Mave walked to the back of the home where she found Jolene separating peas from their pods on the back porch.

"Jolene!" Mave called out from the shaded side of the porch.

"Hey gal, come on up 'ere," Jolene said and then asked, "Whatchu need?"

"I wanted to give you these programs for the church barbecue this weekend," Mave said and handed the programs to Jolene.

"Jist set them there. My hands are wet."

Jolene looked at the programs.

"Hold one of 'em up, so I can see it real good," Jolene said.

Mave held up one of the programs.

"Oh, this is nice Mave. Looks professional," Jolene said.

"Thanks, it took no time at all."

"Wow, how did ya get this so lined up?" Jolene asked while looking at the heading of the program.

"I use'ta work on the yearbook in high school."

"Yeah, Duck mentioned that."

While Mave managed to get over her new awkwardness in dealing with Jolene, Jolene was not quite sure about Mave or Mave's motives. They were friendly, and when the girls were around, they both enjoyed a good gossip. The one thing they never discussed, though, was Shirley.

As the wealthiest wife among their set, Jolene naturally set the tone of conversations in the group, and on most occasions she managed to control the group's dynamics. On this particular afternoon, the conversation would continue in the same way others had.

"Mave, can I ask you somethin'?" Jolene asked, looking down into the bowl of peas.

"Yes, whatchu need, Jolene?"

"Does me being married to Duck bother you?"

"Why no, why would it?" Mave asked.

"Come on, Mave, I know you and Shirley are very close."

"She's been my closest friend since I was a little girl."

"I know but I married her beau, and I know it must bother you some."

"Actually, Shirley didn't wanna get married," Mave said and then added, "At least not to Duck. No offense." Jolene did not say anything because she was unsure whether Mave was just being mean or presenting the truth of Shirley's situation.

Mave did not realize the impact of her words on Jolene until Jolene said, "I'm sorry. I wasn't trying to say anything. It's just—I like you. I think we gotta lot in common and—"

Before Jolene finished, Mave said, "Jolene, all I was sayin' is that there is nothin' for you and I to be uncomfortable about where Shirley is concerned. She didn't wanna git married." Mave smiled and then said, "I already thought we were friends, but okay."

Glad that they were on good footing again, Mave sat next to Jolene on the stoop and helped her with the peas.

Chapter Twenty – Typhoons

Heading back toward Macon and her other life, Shirley's only thought was, "Home just isn't home anymore." She passed all of her childhood haunts—the pond, the movie theater, and the strip mall—and then she went further into the country. When she arrived at the depot, loneliness enveloped her like never before. For the first time since she left home, she felt isolated from everything she held close to her.

On her way to the Pacific, she thought over her decision to leave. At the time it was a great decision, but sitting on the plane on the way to Japan, she worried whether in running away from marriage she had left her life as well. When she reached Okinawa, tired from the excessive travel, she met with her sponsor briefly and settled in for the evening. The next couple of days after arriving on the island, she organized her life. She made rank the previous year and would be working the same job, but her responsibilities had changed slightly. She also prepared herself to go back to school. After speaking with Mave, her desire to finish school had intensified. She wanted to go home with accomplishing in part at least one of her goals.

The first course she signed up for was Western Civilization. For the first time she learned of the significance of the marriage contract in Western European history, and she also met Mark Shiraga. Through him, her circle of friends widened. His open, easygoing manner made her comfortable. Watching him, she learned the fine art of small talk. She learned to carry on lengthy conversations that were almost always about nothing. She also learned to cook in a new way. Gone were the small tubs of butter and lard, and instead she used peanut and sesame oil to flavor a meal. She also realized that soy sauce and teriyaki would do the same thing as meat drowned in gravy. Additionally, she picked up kayaking and waterskiing, in addition to surfing, while hanging out with Mark. With Mission Beach being close at hand, the beach became her island getaway and her weekends became consumed with leisure.

More importantly, Mark allowed her to be herself. His sensitivity toward her attracted her to him even more. He felt the same way about her but for other reasons. No concept or idea was foreign to her. He especially liked that she had very few hang ups, and he could share himself in a way he had not with other girlfriends. Many of their conversations ran along the same quiet tempo of reasoning and then amicable resolution. In more comfortable times, they even went as far as discussing a future together.

"So, do you plan to ever get out of the military?"

"Eventually, I guess," she answered. "Do you have family in the states?"

"Yes, cousins and uncles." He added, "But my immediate family has been in Okinawa my entire life."

"Would you consider livin' in the United States?" Shirley asked.

"The few times I've been, there was really nothing drawing me to the place, but I would never say no."

He then asked, "Would you ever consider living here?" He peered over her head. The two of them were nestled on a blanket facing the ocean's expanse with Shirley sitting in front of him.

"Probably not, but I try not to rule anything out."

She stared at the other beachgoers. Mark lifted the tip of her chin and kissed her ever so lightly on the lips. It was the sweetest kiss ever, and the kiss began Shirley's second attempt at romance. Their passion for each other grew from a mutual respect of ideas. On one occasion, though, just before bedtime, the two were in bed talking about rituals, one of the topics in their religion class. Shirley knew there was a difference in the way they were raised, but when he asked her about Duck, the full reality of what she had done in Hickshaw consumed her thoughts.

"Why did you run from your first husband?" Mark asked in a soft voice.

Shirley stumbled over her words because she never considered Duck seriously as a life partner. Mark was an American, but he was also Japanese, and he did not look at her leaving in the same way. In his world, disobeying a parent was one of the most dishonorable acts a child could commit against a parent. While his American-born mother might understand, he could not imagine disappointing his father. Shirley knew they would have this conversation one day, and she would have to explain this serious breach of trust with her parents.

"I left because I was too scared and young for marriage."

"You disobeyed your parents because you were scared?" He asked, his tone becoming more serious.

"I was of my majority. I really didn't consider it disobedience."

Mark sat silently for a while. He did not want to judge her, but Shirley felt his judgment. Never before had she been faced with someone who disagreed with her decision to leave. Many people she spoke to found her actions brave, even courageous. Shirley left Hickshaw for freedom, but Mark doubted her loyalty.

Then he asked, "Do your parents trust you?"

"With most things, yes, I gather they do trust me. Why wouldn't they?"

Mark tried to find the right words while not offending Shirley. He ignored her last comment and then asked, "Do you know what filial piety is?"

"Isn't it when a child honors the wishes of their parents regardless of their own desires?"

"Something like that." He continued, "I would've gotten married."

"Even if you knew you weren't ready t'git married? Or that you didn't even love the person enough to marry'm?"

"Even if I wasn't ready or I was not in love. My parents know me well enough to know what is good for me. I trust that. Plus, I don't know. If I can't be loyal to my parents, how can I be loyal to another person?"

"I don't think me honoring my right as a free person by not honoring a marriage, which would have been a farce as far as I am concerned, negates any loyalty that I may have to a potential mate," Shirley said and continued to explain in earnest, "Plus, my parents know me as well, but I just didn't want their lives."

"You come from a good family, don't you?" Mark asked.

"Well, yeah."

"Then, why wouldn't you want your parents' lives?"

"I don't know," Shirley said and then she added, "I just want to see the world before I commit myself like that. It's very important that I know who I marry and I wouldn't have had I got married outta high school."

Both of them remained quiet, with Shirley becoming fearful that this conversation would begin the end. They had not expected this one divergence in thought to be the crack in what was a seemingly good relationship. They had been dating almost two years when they had this conversation. They went to sleep and continued relating to each other, never mentioning the conversation again. However, something in the relationship had changed, and as their relationship approached the two-year mark, Mark made excuses as to why he could not spend time with her. Shirley thought he might be seeing someone else, but never in the time they were together had he given her any reason to not trust her. Not until they were out on the beach with a group of Mark's friends from high school did all Shirley's suspicions become realized.

"So when will you tell her?" asked Chris, Mark's friend from elementary school.

"Soon, because my parents have already started planning for April."

"You shouldn't play around with her. She's nice, even you said."

"I know. That's what I hate about this. She is actually good," Mark said.

"You should tell her soon. She's beginning to look at you like they do when they get too serious. Plus, it's not fair." Standing outside of the beach bathroom waiting for a stall to open, Shirley heard pieces of the conversation, not quite knowing what to expect, but expecting the relationship would end soon.

Even with her hearing this conversation, Shirley never saw it coming. On the same spot on Mission Beach where he delicately kissed her and declared his love two years earlier, his words sliced into her like a knife, the blade's sharpness tapping into a pain even Shirley did not think she could endure.

"I'm engaged," he said.

"What?" she asked. His announcement threw her for a loop her because she thought he might propose as his voice, while nervous, was sincere, the serious tone many men get when they are going to announce something important.

In shock, the only words Shirley heard was, "I love you," and "filial piety," "number one son," "dishonor my parents," "I didn't find out until a couple of weeks," and "was promised to her in my teens."

Tears running down her face, Shirley pulled away from his embrace and said, "Why didn't you tell me as soon as you knew about her?"

"I didn't know I would fall this deeply in—I didn't know." He added, "This is something that can't be changed. I'm sorry."

"Just leave me. Please just go."

He hesitated. "I don't want you to stay here outside by yourself. It's going to get cold, and soon you'll be the only one on the beach."

Shirley smiled through her tears and said, "I'll be fine. Please just go. You have no idea how you've just hurt me."

Mark left. Dusk was approaching and there was more darkness in the sky than light. Shirley sat in the sand reflecting on her own failed arranged marriage. She remembered the day clearly. Both sets of parents at Patsy's were in one booth and she and Duck in the other. Shirley had no idea what was taking place until the ride home.

"You and Duck seemed to be getting along," her mom said. Shirley sat quietly, her thoughts on the upcoming spring dance.

"He really seems to have taken to you," her mother continued.

"Mama, Duck has been in every class with me since the first grade."

"What do you think about marriage?" her father asked.

"I dunno. Haven't really thought about it."

"Would you be interested in marrying Duck?" her father asked.

"I don't love him like that."

"Well, what do you plan on doin' after high school? You can't live with us forever," her mother said.

"I know."

"Think on it. You might change your mind," her father said. Shirley put the whole idea of marriage away until her father came back a few days later.

"It's been settled. The two of you'll marry this summer," her parents said, deciding for her.

Shirley never had the opportunity to say no, and it never entered her mind to just obey them. The minute she was told about her impending marriage she did not call Mave, who was in the throes of her own predicament. She called Jamie. He suggested the military.

Shirley did not really think about Duck much these days, but now facing the cool Pacific winds, she was comforted in the thought that she came across the world to find she made the right decision. After Mark left, she sat on the beach, the fall breeze gently nudging her to leave the spot that, up until this point, had been one of the few pleasures she had. A few months after Mark's announcement, she happened to see him and his visibly pregnant wife at the Base Exchange. Shirley was waiting to pay on her stereo on layaway when she saw him standing in line, his wife in front of him full with pregnancy. Mark saw her, but she avoided his eyes. When the customer service representative called her number, she paid on her eight-track player and walked out of the door, feeling his penetrating gaze follow her out of the store.

Chapter Twenty-One – Flowers

Francesca walked into the apartment she shared with Jamie and found a dozen roses sitting on the dinette in the cramped kitchen. Jamie sat on the loveseat and watched Gunsmoke on American Forces Network.

"Oh, I see you've been watching my father again," Francesca said.

"Why do you say that?" Jamie asked, half-distracted by the television noise.

"The roses. My father gives my mother roses every Sunday. I don't know why he's so devoted to giving them. He's so inconsiderate of her in other ways."

"It was a gesture. I'd thought you'd like it," Jamie said. Jamie and Francesca had argued about money the night before, and he did not know what else to do to make it right but to buy flowers.

"Thanks," she said abruptly.

"You're welcome," Jamie said. Francesca walked back to the bedroom and placed her shopping bags in the bedroom. The apartment remained quiet with only the sounds of the television and Francesca rustling with her bags filling the space with noise.

Jamie walked to the back of the apartment into the bedroom

where Francesca was and asked, "What did you buy?"

"Nothing. Just some things to wear out."

"Like?" Jamie asked and went to look in one of the bags.

"Like none of your business," she said and snatched the bag out of his hands.

Jamie's feelings were not hurt, but he was concerned that he had said or done something wrong that really bothered her. Instead of trying to talk to her, he watched her walk around the room while changing from her street clothes to more comfortable clothes.

"Okay, Francesca, what is it now?"

"Nothing. Why do you ask?"

"Well, I buy you flowers, and you have nothing to say. Most women would be grateful for a husband who bought flowers for them."

"To make up for something. Jamie, there is more to marriage than buying flowers anyway."

"I know there is, but it's like you're angry at me about something, but you won't just tell me what it is!"

Francesca looked at Jamie and then said, "I don't know. It just seems like you're trying to be my father."

"What's wrong with a man trying to be good to his wife? What, Francesca? I don't understand you sometimes. You come from one of the finest families in Aviano and that I've ever met, but even in this gesture you find fault."

Francesca sat on the bed next to Jamie and looked down on the bedspread.

"You see my father giving my mother roses and you see a devoted husband. All I can see is a man making up to his wife."

"For what? Your father is one of the most respectable men I've ever met."

"You look at my family and you see this one big, happy family. That is not the case. When we were kids, my father used to go to San Giovanni for the weekend, usually Friday and Saturday, but he would be back for Sunday mass. Every Sunday afternoon, without fail, he would go by the street vendor and purchase flowers for Mama."

"I'm still trying to figure out why the flowers I bought upset you."

"Listen. When I was about fifteen, I heard my mother and father talking about a trip we'd take with my father to San Giovanni. It wasn't until a week before my birthday did my father tell me and my brothers and sisters that we'd be meeting Idora."

"Okay."

"She's my half-sister. He told us she was our sister on the way to meeting her. I had no preparation. I couldn't feel anything. She's younger than us. I couldn't be even mad at her for existing. It was just bad for us all around."

"Wow," Jamie said. "I don't know what to say to you." He then asked, "How old is she?"

"She's a couple of years younger than me. I believe now she's eighteen." Francesca then added, "He started an affair with this woman right after my mother became pregnant with my youngest brother."

Jamie looked at her and this picture of her family that he had envisioned changed in a matter of minutes.

She continued, "My family looks perfect, Jamie, but it isn't. You judge your mother and you think the life she has given you isn't good. But at least she was honest with you. My father has left my mother on several occasions to be with this woman, always coming back, always making up."

"Oh, Francesca. I'm sorry. I just assumed—" Jamie said while pulling her into a tight embrace.

"Those flowers he gave to her, while very beautiful, had many thorns," Francesca said and then laid her head on his lap.

Chapter Twenty-two — Scholarship

The orange sky began the onset of evening and the end of the day took in the beauty of the setting sun. After Mave's visit with Jolene that afternoon, Mave drove home mostly in the silence of the car. She was on her way home when she detoured into the Hickshaw High School parking lot. She got out of the car and walked to the gates of the playing field. Standing outside of the locked gates, Mave walked to its opening and slipped between the padlocked fence. She walked once around the track and then took a seat on the bleachers. Seeing Jolene made her crave the freedom she relinquished a few years earlier. Going over every milestone in her life, Mave arrived at the evening of the awards ceremony, an evening that turned her life around.

"We'd like everyone to be quiet until all the awards have been passed out," the principal said, and then he passed the microphone to the dean of students, who began to call the names off and eventually he reached Mave's name.

"Mave Michaleson was awarded a scholarship for $500 to Hickshaw Junior College."

Her parents were glad their daughter, with her book smarts, would be able to fund, in part, her own education. Shirley was excited that Mave would finally get the honor of valedictorian, an honor Mave had competed for four years to win. No one knew who received those scholarships until that night, making the announcement that much sweeter. She took a moment to reflect on the congratulations everyone gave her as she held the certificate in her hand. Teachers, classmates, and family all stood in line to wish her the best of success.

A car horn blared in the distance waking her up out of the daydream she was having about this important night. She thought more about that evening. After the awards ceremony, both families—Mave's and Shirley's—went to Patsy's to celebrate. They finished eating around eight o'clock when Gus picked Mave up for a movie.

Gus had not really pressured her. She loved him. They had been friends in school since junior high. When she told him about the scholarship, he seemed happy because she would not be going too far, as the junior college was just around the corner.

"You plan on startin' this fall?" Gus asked.

"That's the plan so far. I havta get a job because the scholarship is for a semester and books will be expensive," she explained. She continued, "That's what Mrs. Hodsteter said."

"Mmmmm," he said running over in his head what her achievement would mean to his place in her world. He then added, "Good for you. Ole' Mave Michaelson is gonna be an educated woman."

With Gus, it was more than love. He adored Mave. He did not want to take the chance that maybe some intellectual with long hair and sandals would turn her thoughts around about him. He did not know how else to keep her from leaving. Gus did not mean to get her pregnant, but he knew coming across a girl like Mave was rare, and if they slept together at least once, she would find it very difficult to leave.

To celebrate her achievement, he got his older brother to purchase some Blue Ribbon beer and took her to the lake, where they sat on the picnic benches sipping the cheap beverage.

"So what are the plans 'bout us?" he asked in a hushed voice.

"Well, I love you. You know that," she answered quietly.

"What about marriage?" he asked.

Mave hoped he would not do this, not a proposal, because really she had plans. She was going to see the world, to become a journalist with one of the big stations on the six o'clock news reporting on events and interviewing international dignitaries. At this point in her education, she really did not think there was a choice between him and school. Gus moved closer to kiss her, and she kissed him back. Something in his kisses told her he wanted to be with her, not to just kiss her. She did not stop him because something in her wanted him in the same way. Before they knew it, they were back in the truck both quietly reflecting on what occurred.

"Are you cryin'?" Gus asked.

"Oh Gus, I'm not a virgin anymore," she wept.

"Honey, I'm gonna marry ya. Stop cryin'."

"Still, we shouldn't have done that. We should have waited, and I dunno if I even wanna get married."

Mave turned to look out of the car window. When Gus dropped her off at the house, Mave used the rearview mirror to make sure she was in order before stepping out of the car. The next couple of weeks were nail-biters. Mave could time her cycle to the second, and when the red river did not show, fear set firmly in her heart.

"Mama," she said after waiting two weeks.

"What?" Mrs. Michaelson said, preoccupied with supper.

"Is it possible to have a baby and go to school?"

Mrs. Michaelson dropped the kitchen utensils, walked over to where her eldest daughter sat, and looked into the innocent's wide-eyed gaze.

"What do you mean?" her mother asked.

"I think I'm pregnant, Mama," she said.

Her mother took it in and said, "Dear child, what have you and Gus done?" She continued, "We'll have to see if you're really pregnant."

Going to the doctor was just a perfunctory task because Mave already knew. The conversation with her parents had been easier compared to Gus.

"We havta get married," he said.

"What? Gus, we are too young!"

"That's the right thing, Mave."

"Gus, I wanna go to school," Mave said, wanting to scream but using her most even, patient tone with him.

"Mave, you know how these people are. I don't want them lookin' at my child and heapin' all kinda insults on him because we didn't marry." He begged, "Please don't think about doin' anything by yerself. I've gotta job with my father. We'll be all right."

When Gus and Mave ran it by both sets of parents, they were almost relieved. No shame. They had been dating seriously close to a year, so a May wedding was really no surprise announcement. That was close to three years ago, and she wondered whether she would ever get back on track. The slight breeze caressed her cheek, drying tears she did not feel until she was about to leave the stadium. She wiped the wetness from her face and drove home, painfully aware of the opportunity she sacrificed to be good. Not until the following fall when Mrs. Waverly from the high school library approached her about volunteering a few hours a week did Mave see the platform that could springboard her into school. When she was in school, she liked being in the library because she was surrounded by knowledge. As a volunteer, she worked five hours a week and on Fridays. She first learned how to check books in and out, and then she learned to restack them in a timely fashion. While Mrs. Waverly taught students library skills, Mave cataloged and helped with checking books out.

Mave did not tell Gus about volunteering at the library. She got around daycare because Chet was old enough to attend school, and her mother watched Lux for the five hours she was supposed to be running errands. She kept this secret from Gus because it was something that she herself owned and because she did not want to have any protracted arguments as to why she wanted to volunteer. Just before Lux was born, she figured sometimes it was just better to do whatever she wanted quietly to keep the peace. When she volunteered, this time was one of the happiest times in Mave's marriage. She had freedom and she could pretend for once she did not have a family. She could be the young intern or the college student for summer hire, but she was free.

Mave had been working in the library for about two months when an old high school running buddy, Phillip Watson, began his student teaching at the school. He just happened to run into Mave as she was running an errand for the head librarian.

"Mave Michaelson, is that you?" asked Phillip. Mave turned slowly. He had matured so much she barely recognized him.

"Phillip, how are you?"

"Fine. Boy, it's good to see you. I've been home since the summer, and it seems everyone is still off at school or hitched," he said jokingly.

"Well, I'm married—Mave Henriksen."

"You and Gus married?"

"Yep, right after school let out."

"Well, it's good to see you," he said. "I'm here doing my practicum."

"What's a practicum?"

"Student teaching," he explained.

"Okay. Well, I'm on an errand. We can talk later!" Mave asked and nudged him on the shoulder.

Mave found Watson's presence comforting, as he was a nice surprise from the old days. Mave had changed so much that the days of high school football games and marching bands seemed a distant vision in her rearview mirror, and for once, she did not feel so bad that someone had achieved the one thing she still so desired. She had known he won a scholarship to the University of Georgia, but what she had not known was he spent one semester in Mexico brushing up on Spanish and that he made the Dean's list all four years he was in college.

When she told him about the life she and Gus built together, he could only say, "Boy, time does surely pass. Mave, it really just seems like yesterday we were kids."

"I know," she said, reflecting on his statement.

He had been there about four months when Mave joined him for lunch. He was at one end tucking into his chicken salad sandwich ravenously, and she was on the other end nibbling on a little snack she brought for herself. They moved beyond the small pleasantries of the first few weeks and actually became somewhat good friends.

"Phillip," Mave said. He acknowledged her in between bites.

"Do you have a girlfriend?" Mave did not know why she asked that question. He just seemed like a nice, handsome person. She could not picture him by himself.

"I've dated. But no, right now, I don't have a girlfriend," he said. He looked her in the eye and then asked, "Do you have someone in mind?"

Nervously she said, "No, it just seems—You're so nice. Why wouldn't you?"

"Why wouldn't I be married?"

"Well, yeah."

"The last girlfriend I dated in school left for France. I might've married her, but really the thought never entered my mind."

He continued, "Mave, let me ask you—why did you marry? I don't mean to pry, but you had a scholarship. I thought you were going to college. That's where everybody thought you were headed." Up until this point, no one questioned why she married Gus.

In a moment of perfect clarity and truth, she blurted out, "I got pregnant." They both sat quietly for a minute and then Mave elaborated, "I was supposed t'go to school, but I got pregnant."

Phillip did not know what to say, but he felt an intense wave of regret and sadness coming from Mave. She had not said anything in particular, but the way in which she had unfolded the last five years of her life in those few words told him life had not been the fairy-tale picture painted for outsiders, at least for Mave it had not been.

"Really, it's not so bad," she said.

"You don't have to talk about it if you don't want to," Phillip said.

"I love Gus. If I had my druthers I would have gone to school, but it just didn't turn out that way for me," she explained.

Phillip did not want her to cry, but sensing she was about to, he ever so lightly took his hand and placed it on hers.

"You can still go to school. There are so many ways, and with you being married you shouldn't have to worry about childcare."

"I'll work it out," she said through a pinched smile.

As innocent as this interaction was for both Mave and Phillip, Mave learned firsthand the hazards of crossing boundaries in this town. He barely touched her hand. She saw nothing lustful or adulterous in what had happened. However, someone from the school kept tabs on her and her interactions because one evening Gus came home, and there was a tightness in his voice she did not recognize. At dinner, he said nothing throughout the entire meal, and this treatment continued in this way for about a week when after church he declined his in-laws' invitation to eat.

Gus told Mave, "We need to talk."

She asked her mother-in-law to watch the kids for a couple of hours while she and Gus took care of some personal matters.

"Is everything alright?" Mrs. Henriksen asked. All Mave could do was shrug a tentative yes because she did not know what was wrong. Over at Patsy's, Mave ordered a salad and Gus ordered in such a solemn voice the same meat loaf dinner special she could make for him at home.

Mave said, "All right, Gus, you've got me here waitin' in anticipation. What is goin' on with you?"

"What do you mean?"

"What do you mean what do I mean?" She continued, "Gus, you've barely said more than three sentences to me since last week."

Gus simply asked, "How's Phillip?"

The sting of being caught in not only lying about volunteering but also in whatever Gus suspected was going on with Phillip appeared in the flush redness of Mave's countenance.

"I—I—I don't know. What do you mean?" she asked.

"Mave, we can't keep secrets. We just can't. Please tell me you haven't done anything with that boy," he pleaded.

"Gus, all I do is volunteer at the library a coupla hours a week. That's all. I eat lunch with Phillip when I have a break."

"Where are my children when you are doin' this?"

"The kids are fine. I don't leave them with Mama for more'n

four hours," she answered shortly. She looked across the table and saw Gus was not happy with the explanation she had given him, so she continued. "Gus, I need life. I gotta get out that house for a coupla hours a day or I'm gonna go crazy."

He placed his fork on his plate and slid into the booth next to her.

"Why didn't you just tell me that's what you were doin'?" He continued, "Do you know how ridiculous I look when someone says to me, I saw your wife with that Phillip Watson sharin' intimacies at the school. Hell, Mave, I didn't even know you were workin' at the school, and then I hear this. I shouldn't have had to stand there with my mouth wide open and no explanation."

"Why do you even havta explain anything?"

"It's how it looks, Mave."

"God, I wish people would just tend to their own affairs. It would make my life easier. If anyone told you I was sharin' intimacies, they flat out lied, Gus." Mave continued, "I'm over there volunteerin' in the library, and Phillip and I just talk. I need to have somethin' outside the family. It's innocent." She looked searching his eyes.

He faced her and said, "Please, I love you. Don't keep secrets like that from me. We're married, Mave. Married people don't hide stuff from each other."

Gus slid back over to the other side of the booth and finished his meat loaf. On this day, Mave learned her leash had not been lengthened by much. She was young and still tempting. Nothing sets a town a fire more than some salacious tidbit about a young wife stepping out on her husband. Although she knew people in town to be small-minded and petty as to interfere in the one relationship she cultivated beside the one with Jolene, she did not realize she was being scrutinized so closely. To satisfy Gus, she moved the time she volunteered for the school to a day when Phillip was not there. Gus did not make a big deal about the volunteering because this was the first time he felt a real crack in their relationship. He was in it for the long haul and did not want to risk losing Mave over a few hours at the school library.

Chapter Twenty-three — Town Soup

Shirley had been gone almost five years, and the one Christmas she did get to spend at home two years earlier, had been tempered by her own anxiety about finding her place in a community that had all but moved on without her. Mave, on the other hand, found Christmas holidays to be fun and a break from the routine of her life as a mother and wife.

This year, the Chamber decided to hold the annual Town Soup in the high school gym, as it had been a bitter, cold winter and not too many people could stand the freezing temperatures. Town Soup was held every Christmas Eve, and it was an event where everybody in the town, regardless of race or religion, gathered to partake of the soup served that year. Because these were country people, the ingredients came from what was available in the pantries of the women who gathered to cook the meal. Of course there was other food, but the main course was the soup, which was usually served with hearty grain bread some of the women decided to bake that year.

Mave would participate with her mother, and so would a now grown and engaged Marla. Jolene was there, and so were some of the girls from high school who had since married. Shirley's mother joined Mave's mother and some of the older women in cutting up the vegetables while the younger wives helped with setting up the tables for the crowds that would gather. At about 6:00 p.m., the first few families trekked in and by 7:30 p.m. the high school gym had been alive with Christmas revelers. When everyone served themselves, Mave, Marla, Jolene, and some of the other young women found themselves a table and enjoyed a bowl of the sustenance while wishing each other a blessed year.

"Marla, I hear you're gettin' married," Coreen, one of Mave's classmates, said.

"By golly," Marla said. "News does travel fast. Joe just popped the question a month ago."

"Yeah, yer mother was tellin' us about it while we were in the cafeteria," Coreen said.

Josie, a young woman from Marla's class, said, "Good for you. It's not too good to be settin' 'round without no man to come home to."

Coreen then said, "Speakin' of engagements, how's Shirley?"

While some time had passed, some of the women in Hickshaw wanted to know the details of Shirley's escape, some skirting around the subject and others being very direct. Mave, before this time, never betrayed her friend by making Shirley's reasons for leaving fodder for town gossip.

"Shirley's fine. She's doin' an assignment in Japan," Mave said, hoping this explanation would be the end of this subject.

"She gotta fella?" Josie asked.

"Why, yes, she was seein' this Japanese guy," Mave said.

"Japanese?" Jolene said. "Why, she coulda stayed right here and got married. Why'd she havta to leave the continent, much less for a Japanese boy?"

"She didn't leave for a Japanese boy," Mave said.

Before she could finish, Coreen said, "No offense, Jolene, but had

Shirley remained in Hickshaw, you woulda not been settin' right there in that seat as Jolene Hanson. No offense."

"I'll try not to be offended by yer callous observation," Jolene said, and then she asked, "You know, Mave, it seems kind of odd, but why on earth did she leave?"

Mave, realizing she would have to answer that question, said, "I guess she's afraid to marry, afraid of sex. Shirley was always a bit shy about boys."

"You mean she's still a virgin?" Marla asked.

"Now, I didn't say that," Mave said.

Jolene asked, "So how many lovers do you think she's had?"

"At least two. You'd a thought with my mistake, she would have kept her legs closed," Mave said. The words flew out of Mave's mouth before she could prevent them from leaving. She met the looks of disproval from the faces of the other women at the table, as up until this point no one except for the people to whom Mave disclosed the information regarding her own nuptials knew she was pregnant before she got married.

Coreen, ignoring the last part of Mave's last sentence, said, "I betcha' it must be real nice having a different lover every night and not having anyone to judge ya for it."

Mave said, "She doesn't sleep around. I only think she's had two boyfriends."

Jolene then said, "Well, Mave, you know she'd done more. She's just not tellin' you anything."

"Thank goodness we're married. We don't havta worry about that sorta thing anymore," Mave said.

"I don't know. She seemed kinda happy when she was home coupla years ago," Marla said.

"Well, she isn't," Mave said. Then she turned to Marla. "Just be glad the first one you done it with wanted to marry ya."

Chapter Twenty-four – A Projection

The first thing Jamie did when he left the restaurant was to go back to the bedroom and close the door. Francesca would be home in an hour, which would give him plenty of time to search her things to find the one thing that would tell him everything. Usually, he would not leave work until just before seven in the evening, and by that time Francesca would already be at home with supper cooked. Today, though, the office was slow and so his supervisor let him go early. He thought he would stop by the restaurant to see if Francesca wanted to eat out instead of dining in. Before he could go into the restaurant, he saw the figure of a man who was familiar to him. He got out of the car to get a closer look, and yes, he was looking at Sincich.

When Jamie married Francesca, he not only made sure Sincich was out of the picture, he made sure Sincich knew he was no longer going to be a part of Francesca's life. However, seeing Sincich in the parking lot only fueled his worries about the state of his marriage. Instead of going into the establishment, he left because he did not know what to do.

When he opened the diary, the letter slipped out of the binder. He opened the letter and read its contents. Jamie was not really hurt by Sincich's declaration of love nor was he really surprised, but an angry fire burned at the pit of his stomach. He was actually trying to be a good man to this woman. He imagined, in ten or fifteen years, Francesca and he would have a large family of their own if he could convince her to conceive. For the forty-five minutes he had to think, he cooked supper and tried to rationalize why another man would write his wife, to find some logical reason that would negate Francesca's betrayal of him. At half past five o'clock, Francesca walked into the apartment.

"Mmmm, smells good. Got off early?" Francesca said.

"Yes."

"What did you make?" Francesca asked.

"A little chicken, some mashed potatoes."

"Southern. Sounds good. I'll set the table."

"I've already set it in the dining room," Jamie said.

Francesca showered and changed. She walked into the dining room where Jamie had already been seated.

"Oh, this is so cozy. You keep doing this and I might have to keep you around," she said and chuckled slightly.

Jamie remained quiet. Francesca felt the coolness in his demeanor when she walked into the house, but she chalked it up to him having a difficult day. In this moment, she felt the chill more acutely. In more comfortable moments, she would say something funny to break the ice, but this time nothing would open the door to his warmth.

"Actually, me and you, we have something to discuss," Jamie said. Jamie did not have the words to tell her what he needed, and so he slid the letter across the table toward her. She immediately recognized the stationery.

"You've been through my things," she said in an accusatory tone.

"Yes, I saw him go into the restaurant today, Francesca."

Francesca did not need to know whom Jamie saw because she already knew. Even though she told him she would stop talking to Sincich, she had not but she was still angry with Jamie for going through her journal. Francesca got up from the table, forgetting to push in the chair. She ran to the bedroom and then returned to the dining room with the diary in her hand.

"Here read this too, Jamie, if you must know my every thought," she said and pointed to an entry in the small journal dated the week she received the letter. The entry was short, but it said everything he needed to know.

"What does it say, Jamie?"

Jamie did not say anything.

"No, dear husband, what does it say?"

In the meekest voice a man could have, Jamie read the sentence, "I've decided to remain committed to my husband, so that is the end of that."

"Jamie, you're the one with the commitment problem—not me!" she said and stormed off to the bedroom with the diary and the letter in her hand.

Chapter Twenty-Five — A Midafternoon Wedding

Church that Sunday had been a special treat for Mave because Marla and her fiancé announced their plans for a wedding. The couple almost seemed perfect. Marla met Joe in Sunday school two years earlier. She always thought of his needs first and vice versa. He was slightly older than she was, and he was in the process of completing his second year at the junior college. Marla planned to join him after graduation. When people thought of them, they often did as a staple in the community.

Like Mave, Marla's wedding was planned for the middle of spring, and Mave was excited because she knew her mother would get a thrill from seeing at least one of her daughters properly married. Marla had decided on her bridesmaids early on. Mave was Marla's matron of honor, and Mave did not skip a beat when Marla requested her help in organizing the wedding.

The day of the wedding, Mave made a special trip to the church and to the reception hall to see if everything was ready. The church was decorated beautifully. Marla did not want anything too flashy. Ultimately, she decided on pale lavender for the color scheme and a lot of pink flowers. They planned for an outdoor wedding, so the trees and surrounding greenery were a perfect complement to the colors chosen for the event. As a midafternoon and evening affair, everyone would enjoy the splendor the evening stars would have on the reception hall deck. Making her rounds to the reception hall, Mave paid close attention to the decorations, making sure everything was perfect.

Mave meticulously made the bride and groom centerpieces that dotted each table, light lavender accenting the bride and groom encased in a glass fixtures. Atop the fixture were small tea lights in different scents. The hall must have been used for cotillions and coming-out balls because of the small walkway in the center, and it had a dance floor fit for royalty. Mave had never seen anything so fancy in her life. If the inside was something to imagine, the outside was breathtaking and majestic. At night, the stars lit up the sky illuminating the deck and the lake. Just before the wedding, Mave brought Marla and Joseph over at night so they all could take in this beauty together.

The day of the wedding Mave spent the morning putting the finishing touches on the decorations at the church. At about ten o'clock, Mave went home and put herself together. Her own wedding was a far cry from the organized and well-thought-out affair that would take place that evening. Mave faced the mirror and the image of the protruding stomach crashed in on the memory. Stepping out of this portrait, Mave finished dressing and joined Gus and the kids in the truck. They were to meet Marla and their parents at the church at eleven that morning. Marla was at the church, her gown an exquisite white with a slip of lavender and her hair was done up in a French twist with cascading curls.

Everyone was told the wedding would start sharply at two in the afternoon. The guest arrived and were seated beginning right after one. At a quarter to two, Mave peeked out into the church. Joseph's parents and some of his groomsmen were chatting idly, but there was no Joseph.

They waited and at two, Mrs. Michaelson went into the church hallway and pulled one of the groomsmen aside.

"Where's Joseph?" Marla's mother asked.

"I don't know. Last we saw him was last night," the young man said.

She was not so much worried, but concerned. Joe was a good boy, and she had heard tales of the mischief these boys got into the night before their wedding.

Sensing her discomfort, the groomsman said, "Mrs. Michaelson, we dropped him off last night at home. He should be fine. I swear."

Mrs. Michaelson went back into the anteroom where the bride and her party waited to no avail. The hands on that grandfather clock clicked away slowly as two-thirty turned into three, and by the time they realized it, it was four o'clock. Joseph was not coming. Mr. Michaelson, fed up with what he felt was being turned into a circus, went out into the church audience.

"Folks, I'm sorry, but there isn't gonna to be a church wedding t'day," he said.

A low murmur enveloped the church, and the invitees slipped out of their pews. Soon after, the wedding party left the two families alone at the church. At about seven o'clock, the church sat silent, only an echo of what happened that afternoon hung in the air. Mave and Gus followed her parents, and Marla sat in the backseat of the car, not knowing whether to feel humiliated or worried because they still did not know what happened to Joe. As much as Marla tried to cry, the tears would not come. She could only wonder why he abandoned her. When they reached the Michaelsons' four bedroom home, Joseph sat on the porch steps in a pair of denim jeans and a lumberjack shirt, smelling like Old English aftershave.

Her father charged at him and said, "Boy, what kinda fool are you tryin' to make 'ah my family?" He was about to hit him, but Gus, Mave, and her mother stepped in between them.

"Joe, just go, get outta here. We can talk about this tomorra," Mrs. Michaelson said sharply, her anger contained.

"I can't, Mrs. Michaelson. I can't. I'm leavin'," and then Joseph turned to Marla and said, "I'm leavin'. I need to speak with you."

The once-betrothed couple left the incensed father and confused relatives on the porch. Gus and the Michaelsons went inside, but Mave stayed on the porch. All she heard were the muffled sounds of a jilted bride's angst and the pleadings of a foolish, would-be groom. The enormity of what Shirley had done hit Mave, even though it was not the same. At least Shirley had the good sense to leave before the wedding. When Marla finished with Joseph and he drove off, she sat next to Mave on the stoop and cried such a deep and mournful cry that it scared Mave. Eventually, Mrs. Michaelson came out to comfort her baby girl. Mave and Gus went home and settled in for the night, both holding each other close in the warmth of their small trailer wholly understanding the fragility of relationships, especially their own.

Gus, feeling Mave's pain, kissed her on the forehead and said, "This will blow over and Marla will soon be on her way."

"I don't know. When she was out there on that stoop, ah, Gus, I could have cried a million tears with her. It was so sad. I don't think she'll recover anytime soon."

She did. The next day Marla picked herself up, drove to Macon, and enrolled in school to be a cosmetologist. When she told Mave her plans, her sister's response surprised her.

"Why, I thought you were goin' to school—to college."

"I am. I've just changed fields and locations," Marla said. She then added, "This is just until I figure out what I really wanna to do."

"What's wrong with college?" Mave asked.

"Mave, you know as well as I that I can't stay here."

"So what? Who cares what people think?"

"Mave, I really loved Joseph. Every time I go to that church, anytime I go anywhere in this town, I'll be facin' these people, not to mention his family, who only know, Marla got stood up at the altar. I'm not sure I wanna be that person forever."

"Yer not married—so what? Marla, do you realize the opportunity you've been given?" Mave asked. Marla's face softened, and she reached to touch Mave's hands.

"It's so easy for you to say that, Mave. You never wanted to marry." Her soft but sharp words stung, and all Mave did was purse her lips.

"You be careful in Macon," Mave said and kissed her sister on the cheek.

Two years later, Mave's anger about their world really flared. Joseph Wallace and his wife were properly introduced to the congregation. Mave sat in quiet revolt as the preacher welcomed them into the community and began his sermon. On the ride home, she let her feelings be known to Gus.

"While my sister is in exile, this thing comes crawling back to the community with his new wife and they just accept them." She continued with her rant, "Nevermind that he destroyed my sister and made a joke of our entire family."

"I don't know, it just seems like folks might want a little peace," Gus said, trying to excuse the slight. He continued. "You know, Mave. I don't know if you know this, but there are a lot of people who believed your sister to be prideful."

"What?" Mave asked exasperated. "Gus, I can't believe you entertained that ridiculous thought. My sister did absolutely nothin' to deserve the treatment that boy heaped on her! Absolutely nothing!"

Gus said, "Oh, I know. Marla's my sister too. I was there with you watchin' her crawled up like some baby cryin' her eyes out. I wouldn't wish that upon anyone." He continued, "I'm just sayin' that's how a lot of these people saw the situation."

Gus had never, since they had been married, seen his wife so worked up over anything, and he agreed in their small world sometimes people were judged by the situation they were in instead of their character. Gus had enough of Hickshaw. The months that followed he worked diligently in preparation for their move closer to Macon. The Wallace boy's reintroduction into the community was the incentive Gus needed to move him and his family out of town.

Chapter Twenty-six — Lavender

After Mark left Shirley, she felt a vacuum of time and space in her life, as up until this point Mark consumed her life. However, without him, her life became a series of tasks she compelled herself to complete, and whether or not it involved going to school or work, she stayed busy to avoid thinking about him. Shirley could not figure out what she had done wrong in dating, so ultimately she decided to abstain from dating, which also was a comfort to Mave.

"I don't blame you." Mave continued, "You know, with everything that happened with my sister. Who can fault you for not wantin' to be bothered?"

"I'm tryin' not to see this as such a negative. It's not me tryin' to avoid men because inherently they're bad, but me trying to find out what it is I want," Shirley said.

"What's inherently?" Mave asked and continued, "Nevermind. You know who's workin' at the school?"

"No, who?"

"Phillip Watson." Mave continued, "Yeah, did his practicum there, and they liked him so much they asked him to work full-time after he graduates."

Not much into town going-ons anymore, Shirley asked, "So how are you and Gus?"

"We're about to move closer to Macon." She continued, "He feels the move will do us good."

"I think they're gonna make me do a tour in Korea," Shirley interrupted.

"Really? I'm so excited for you," Mave said. Shirley did not say anything because she knew that these assignments were not the most valued.

"It's just for a year, though. Then, I'm hopin' to come stateside," Shirley said. Shirley received word soon after she completed her associates. This time there was no excitement because her plans for that year were to learn her job better and transfer into a four-year program.

Korea made it easy for her to grow. She had the good fortune to have as a supervisor, TSgt Sherry McGowan, who taught Shirley the importance of using good sense, a skill she would carry throughout her lifetime in the military. Often, their daily work would include conversations where McGowan shared advice she picked up along the way.

"Keep it simple," she advised after Shirley spent the entire morning on a task that probably should have taken an hour. The sergeant continued, "In all things you do, you should try to keep it simple."

Shirley did not understand what her supervisor meant, but this motto was very apparent in McGowan's life. While other service members bought lunch on the economy every day, McGowan brought her homemade lunch. Something pretty special had to be going on for McGowan to spend money for lunch. Instead of spending money on a loaner car, McGowan saved the gas and insurance money and rode her bike to work. Known as a place where people could spend a lot of money, Korea's shopping districts were filled with service personnel spending expensive amounts on souvenirs to send home. Most service members could find great deals by shopping off base rather than the Base Exchange, but McGowan made most of her purchases at the Base Exchange by not buying on time or shopping frivolously. In her leisure, she also did not spend ungodly amounts of time and money at the local hangouts. She was always visiting some place where she could have a "tangible learning experience."

"You see these guys who go to the local bars," McGowan said to Shirley one afternoon. Many service members became distracted with the temporary diversions that overseas assignments offered. Shirley knew what McGowan was talking about because she had already heard the tales of drunken servicemen acting all out of sorts, and some were sent home to America for serious infractions.

"Yes," Shirley said.

"Well, they consume a good part of their income in those bars with nothing to show for it but a good time," McGowan said. "You don't have to go too far to learn about the people who live here. It's free."

McGowan was right because the next time Shirley went off base to Seomyeon, the city center, she learned that Pusan, or Busan, was named "Kettle Mountain" because it was at the base of a mountain, and Foreigner's Street had been named so because during the war the district had been set up to cater to American service members.

In the winter, when the cold set in, she visited some of the historical and cultural monuments like the Beomeosa Temple and the Geumjeongsanseong. Although she had made leisure a top priority in Okinawa, her stay in Korea made her realize the opportunities she missed to learn. Not too many people in Hickshaw were tolerant. Her background was typical of a person growing up in the South in the late sixties, but here in Pusan, she was becoming a woman with a broader worldview. Taking the advice of McGowan, she began to enjoy and learn from her environment.

When she drove to Macon in preparation of military service, she never realized she would become a person whose entire perspective on people would change. In some ways, this search she started years before led her to the same conclusion that people, for the most part, lead the same type of lives. They want to be safe, loved, and respected, regardless of the cultural accoutrements they wore. More importantly, she began to view McGowan as a mentor and not just a commanding officer, as a human being and not just a stereotype. Shirley had been in the military almost seven years, and she knew that finding and keeping good relationships were difficult, and this one she would not discard.

Because she was becoming so cultured, at times when she hung out with her peers she often found herself annoyed or disappointed in their lack of understanding and sophistication. On one particular outing with the girls, Shirley was feeling cultured and decided to counsel her friends on Korean cultural nuances, but she, in turn, would learn something new about her sergeant. When McGowan came into the establishment with a woman, Shirley came into a new understanding about the relationships.

Shirley and a couple of her girlfriends from base decided to go off the installation for dinner. Being the middle of the week, Sun's Korean Barbecue should have been empty. However, the place was filled with customers, some having to wait close to twenty minutes to get a seat. Shirley noticed numerous women in the establishment but made nothing of it. All of the young women at Shirley's table acknowledged McGowan, and then the two girls Shirley was with looked at each other with a knowing glance and snickered.

"What's so funny?" Shirley asked.

"You know whom she's with?" asked one of her friends. Before

Shirley could think about the implication, the other girl piped up,

"Her lover," the young woman said. Both girls waited for the reaction to reach Shirley's innocent face. Instead, a look of confusion and total revulsion appeared on her face.

"They're both women. Do you mean to tell me Sarge is—a lesbian?"

One of the girls interrupted, "It's just salacious rumors and innuendo."

"No, it's not. Remember what Tex said he saw last year?" her friend countered.

The girl did not even acknowledge what the other girl said. She just repeated her earlier phrase, "Rumor and innuendo."

Shirley looked over at the sergeant. She could not fathom that someone she was so close to was homosexual. All of her worries had been confirmed a few weeks later. At work, until she knew exactly who McGowan was, she kept to herself the whole day while trying not to be distracted by thoughts of her supervisor with another woman. They worked this way until one day after work Shirley decided it would be good to get away from the daily scenery of the base. A little coffee shop outside of Pusan was a favorite hangout for Shirley. On her way out of the establishment, she saw McGowan holding the hands of a woman she was seated next to close to the rear of the establishment. At first, she did not think anything of it because it was common for Korean women to hold hands. That was the culture, and when overseas, many Americans adopted the cultural nuances of the host country. However, she had heard the gossip related to McGowan's sexual preference. She did not make her presence known to the two women. Paradoxically, while she felt revulsion, she also felt compassion. She remembered what the people at home did to one of her classmates who was suspected of "being that way."

Sonny Blackwell was an effeminate boy who spoke with a lisp. He hung around girls mostly because many of the boys avoided him. Even though he did not wear women's clothing or appear to like boys, everyone just assumed he was homosexual. The boys and girls at school picked on him to the point of bullying. He did not even wait for graduation. When he turned sixteen, he left Hickshaw. He was supposed to be some big-time art dealer in New York City.

Shirley understood the full implication behind what she saw in the park. Sonny only appeared to be a homosexual and he had suffered the town's disapproval. McGowan was a lesbian. Shirley thought of all the terrible things people would do if they knew about her. Plus, she liked her supervisor, even though she had been taught those types of relationships were an abomination. She never told a soul about what she saw in the shop that day. The following weeks at work she studied her boss, trying to figure it all out. Finally she just got tired of wondering and asked her.

"Sarge. Do you have a boyfriend?"

"Nope," McGowan said sharply. Anticipating the next series of questions, she stated plainly, "I don't date men."

Shirley's ears were ringing and on fire. She could not believe her boss said out loud and so freely that she did not date men. Still, she figured it was best to get as much clarification as possible.

"Do you have a—girlfriend?" she asked.

Tired of all the beating around the bush, McGowan stated in a formal tone, "We're going to have this conversation once," she paused and then continued to explain, "I generally keep my personal business private and separate from my professional affairs, but I sense there is decency in you that will prevent you from getting into the trash talk around here about me."

Shirley just stared at her.

McGowan continued. "Yes, Lorie and I are dating," she said, speaking softly of the woman with whom Shirley had seen her. "Do you have any other questions?"

"Not really." She did, and a lot of them, but in the following weeks Shirley, even though she was confused, got over her discomfort and resumed the relationship she had with her boss. All of the questions she had about McGowan were answered when her supervisor invited her to a get together she was having over the Fourth of July holiday weekend.

Like most single personnel, McGowan elected to live off base. Her apartment had been a mosaic of all the places she had visited in the world. Her walls were adorned with select pieces of artwork and her living room furniture must have been part of a collection, each piece having the signature of the country from which it came. What astounded Shirley was all the types of friends McGowan had, and she was far from the stereotype of whips, chains, and bondage picture Shirley conjured up. McGowan was, by Shirley's standard, very cultured and well put together.

Even though she had been taught what McGowan was doing was a sin and an abomination onto the Lord, she could not ignore that her boss was a strong, independent, and decent human being. Because of these good qualities, whenever her boss's name came up in conversation among her friends, she stayed mum, neither offering up any information to deny or confirm "McGowan's proclivities." Some months after she left Korea, Shirley learned that not only had McGowan begun to openly appear in public with her girlfriend, but sometime after Shirley PCS'd McGowan would also be relieved from active duty with a dishonorable discharge.

Chapter Twenty-seven — Garden Clubs and Cotillions

I'm thinkin' it'd be nice to have gardenias for the cotillion this year. We need a hundred of 'em," Jolene said looking out onto the field that abutted the church grounds.

"Gardenias won't be in season for a' couple of months," Josie said.

"Well, order some. Jesus, you'd a thought there was only one place a flower could grow in Georgia," Jolene said.

This particular evening, the women from the First Episcopal Church of Christ's garden club sat under the live oak discussing the upcoming spring cotillion at the high school. Jean Millingsworth, now Hutchins, got married that cold, brisk February afternoon. Jolene, a woman known to live and breathe town business, on this day felt it necessary to discuss the cotillion after what had been a beautiful ceremony.

"Well, all of us have children, and I, for one, have a daughter. I need to make sure things are done right so when it's her turn it is really good for her too," Jolene said.

Josie said, "Oh, Jolene, Justine is only seven. You have plenty a'time."

"And thank goodness. The young girls today are movin' faster an' faster than ever before. At least we had the common sense to keep our clothes on when we petted. We just didn't give em' everything all at once. Did you hear what that Diedre Wilson did last year?" Coreen said.

"Oh, you mean with that fella from Macon?" Mave asked.

"Yeah, but everybody knows about her havin' that affair with that grown man," Coreen said.

"Isn't she the oldest of the three girls?" Josie asked.

"Yeah," Mave said.

"But let me finish. She had an affair, but the guy was married. Married to some girl, last name's Wright," Coreen said.

"Missy Wright," Mave said. "He was married to Missy Wright."

"What? The boy looked like he could be no more'n twenty-one," Jolene said.

"No, he w'nt that old," Mave said, and then continued, "I use'ta see'm out at the college when Joe and Marla use'ta attend, but that was some years back."

"There aren't any schools in Macon?" Jolene asked.

"I guess some of his peoples are from 'round here. I don't know," Mave said.

"How old is that girl, anyway?" Jolene asked.

"She can't be more'n fourteen," Mave said.

"So what'd her parents do 'bout it?" Coreen said.

"I don't know. They're not from here. I think they sent 'er away. She was preggers. That's how they found out about the boy," Mave said.

Coreen looked at Mave and then said, "Mave, you seemed to have the 411 on this story. I didn't even know the girl was pregn'nt."

"Oh, I made it my business to know just as soon as I saw my Lux playin' with one of the daughters. Can you 'magine havin' to explain to an eight-year-old why her best friend can no longer be her best friend?" Mave said.

Jolene added, "Well, Mave Henrikson, that's got to be about the unkindest thing I've ever seen you do to 'nother person."

"I'm not tryin' to be kind. I'm tryin' to raise a daughter," Mave said.

"You know, Mave isn't entirely wrong about that. 'Member them two gals use'ta cheer for the school when we were in high school, and one ran off with her boyfriend?" Coreen asked.

"Yer talkin' 'bout Mable and Laney," Mave said and then continued, "Yeah, Laney run off with that fella, and soon after Mable turned up preggers."

"It just seems like when one gets the fever, the others follow right along," Coreen said. "Thank goodness I have boys only."

"There are so many things that could steal your child away. A mother would be crazy not to protect her children from those influences," Josie said.

"Well, I know when my Justine gets ready to flower, I'm a set 'er up just like Shirley's mama did," Jolene said.

"Shirley ended up runnin' away," Mave said.

"I'll lock 'er up if she even thinks of runnin'," Jolene said.

"Anyway, you won't have to worry about that because a good man recognizes a good woman on sight. Your Justine and my Lux are bein' raised to be women of excellence, women of quality," Mave said. "Anyway, when men want trash, they'll find it. They won't havta come snoopin' around our daughters."

"You know what, Mave? Yer absolutely right. Anyway, gettin' back to cotillion. Josie, when do you think you can order those flowers?"

Jolene asked.

"Tomorrow mornin', as soon as I get to the shop," Josie said.

The fine ladies of Hickshaw were able to secure themselves enough gardenias so that the junior class of Hickshaw High would have a beautiful, fragrant evening.

Chapter Twenty-eight – Red Light District

When Jamie got the news he would be stationed in Ramstein, Germany, he was glad—glad to be away from Italy and glad to be going somewhere he and Francesca could live and be married without the expectations that both of them placed on themselves. They arrived in Germany during one of the coldest years in the city's history. Since she had never left Italy before, Francesca found herself, for at least the first six months of their assignment, being severely depressed. Because neither she nor Jamie spoke German, they found living on the economy impossible, and so it would be the first time that Francesca would live on base.

Living on base was very different from living on the economy. Because Francesca had felt no need to go on base when they lived in Italy, she did most of her shopping in town for both her grocery and personal items. However, in Ramstein she had no choice but to shop at the commissary, where very few, if any, of the items she was used to cooking with were fresh. Additionally, the Base Exchange offered very little variety in clothing, and Francesca was a clothes hound. Even when some of the more popular styles came into the BX, they were gone as soon as they arrived. Also, the residential communities were almost like small compounds, each having a block monitor and each having restrictions on what could and could not be placed in the yard. Francesca never had her own yard to tend, and her first time was in government housing where she was expected to tend a yard with the threat of receiving a citation if the grass was too high or the yard too unkempt.

Jamie, on the other hand, found Germany refreshing. He needed new scenery, and while Italy was beautiful, he did not miss it as much as Francesca. While their marriage was far from miserable, Jamie felt many of the problems the two shared were related to her being so close to home. On evenings when they would argue, her first instinct would be to go to the restaurant and commiserate with one of her sisters about Jamie's failings while Jamie remained in the apartment wondering when, or if, his wife would come home.

After a year or so, Francesca found a job at the NCO club serving, and in this way, she was able to connect socially with other military wives. Life got a little better for her, as she was able to make friends and learn about the German economy. From these friendships, she learned where to shop on the economy for food, clothing, and other items. She also found great places for her and Jamie to hangout outside of the installation. They became so comfortable with venturing out that when one of Jamie's co-workers told him about a tour bus that took military personnel looking to have fun on the weekends to various cities in Europe, he immediately signed him and Francesca up for a trip to Amsterdam.

Francesca was so excited to go that she could not stop talking about the trip with her friends. They arrived in Amsterdam, and since it was a day trip, Francesca wanted to do as much shopping as possible. By three that afternoon, she was shopped out and exhausted. The pair sat in a small pub and drank refreshments before deciding what to do next.

"You know, let's go see the red light district," Jamie said.

"How much time do we have?"

"The bus doesn't leave until seven," Jamie said.

"Okay, let me finish my beer," Francesca said. The two then walked the mile to the famed district, where they found these bungalows with glass windows. Each window contained a woman—some scantily dressed, some not—who sat waiting for her customers.

"It doesn't really live up to what people say about it," Jamie said.

Francesca said, "Look, Jamie, I think she's looking at you," and she pointed in the direction of a very beautiful, very young woman. Jamie smiled and waved at the young woman. Francesca and Jamie both began to walk in the opposite direction. The young woman knocked on the window, beckoning the both of them.

Francesca said, "Let's see what she wants."

"I know what she wants," Jamie said.

"Come on, let's see," Francesca said.

"What are you saying, Francesca?"

"Nothing, come on," she said and headed in the other direction.

"Francesca, wait!" Jamie said.

Jamie threw away all of his admonitions about family and fidelity and followed her up the steps into the small parlor. One hundred American dollars and an hour later, a surge of shame and embarrassment developed into a blush on Jamie's face. He stared out the window trying to figure out what just happened. Jamie kept looking toward the back of the bus to see the looks of the other day-trippers staring back at him, judging him. He could only imagine what they would be thinking about their actions and what the others back at the base would say.

Sensing his anxiety, Francesca asked him, "You all right?"

"Yes, why wouldn't I be?"

"Jamie, I know you. Look, what we did is our business. Nobody else's. Nobody's going to find out, okay?"

"Okay."

Chapter Twenty-nine—A Bloke

Because of her experience in Korea, when her next assignment—London, England—was given to her, Shirley saw it as an opportunity to learn. In addition to enrolling in night classes, she began to tour the monuments in England. She saw the Crown Jewels, Buckingham Palace, the Changing of the Guard, and Big Ben, and she was ferried down the Thames River. She finally had a good curry, in addition to Jamaican patties, homemade marmalade, biscuits and tea, fish and chips with malt vinegar, and her first taste of British crisps.

Shirley also opened herself to love again. Her roommate, Mitzy Brown, a girl from New York, was a change from any of the women she encountered previously. In the London flat that they shared, Shirley watched Mitzy get ready for dates while she studied for exams.

"Why do you spend so much time in those books?" Mitzy asked Shirley one rainy Saturday when they were both stuck inside.

"I dunno."

"Do you date?" Mitzy asked.

Shirley stared at her animated roommate.

"Are you—that way?" Mitzy asked. "If you are that way, I won't tell. Come on. I have plenty of friends that are lesbians."

"No, I am not that way," Shirley said mocking Mitzy's liberal tone. "I'm on a break from dating."

"Why? You're so pretty—and young." In her thirties, Mitzy had come over to London in her youth to teach students at the American School in London.

Mitzy studied Shirley for a second and then said, "Yes, Shirley Carmichael, we have definitely got to get you out of the house." Through Mitzy, Shirley learned there was an art to dating.

"Don't ever get too deep with them," Mitzy lectured. "Most men just want to have a good time. They don't want to intellectualize and go over deep hurts."

Shaking her finger in front of her face, Mitzy cautioned Shirley, "Don't call them after a date, no matter how much you like them. You don't want to appear desperate."

However, the most valuable pearl she offered to Shirley was, "Sex is never an option."

After the deep hurt of the last few years, Shirley thought burying herself in books was a safe, good thing to do. However, when Mitzy asked about double dating with a fella, Shirley was game. Soon, in addition to the books, Friday and Saturday nights became consumed once again with dating and nightlife.

When Colin Ogelby entered the pub she happened to be frequenting one Friday night, Shirley had no idea how sometimes the rules that work in theory sometimes can go awry in reality. Even though Shirley was reminded of the boys from home when she talked to him, his sincerity threw her for a loop. She was in London two years when they met.

With Colin she could talk freely about her life experiences, which is why when she met him she broke rule one.

"So you work in London?" Colin asked.

"Oh, oh yes."

Getting straight to the point, Colin asked, "Do you have a bloke?"

Shirley smiled and answered, "No."

"Why not?" He asked playfully indignant.

"Because," and then Shirley stopped herself from remembering. "Men don't want to go over deep hurts. They want to have fun."

Colin joked, "I know. I know. It's a long story."

Before they left the pub that evening, Shirley divulged not only her reasons for entering the military but also information about her past two relationships. Up until this point, she had adhered to the rules.

For the most part, she found Colin to be quite delightful. He was originally from Liverpool and came to London to work as a carpenter. Most of his family lived in Liverpool, and so he often left London to visit. Although her attraction to him was not physical, she anticipated his every call. Shirley did not spend too much time worrying about why she liked him so much, so when she began to call him after dates, she did not even let Mitzy's admonishing stares deter her from having a good conversation.

"He's funny and I think he likes me," Shirley explained to Mitzy, but they both knew Shirley was falling in love again.

In the time they dated, Shirley learned the intricacies of rugby, football, and cricket. After attending a few matches, the mania around these sports amazed her. When she talked to Mave, the only way she could describe cricket was, "It's like baseball, 'cept you only have two bases with wickets."

She also fell in love with the English countryside. The pastures were a bright, surreal green, a green she had never seen, even in the most pristine fields in Georgia. In more romantic moments, Colin and Shirley found themselves parked along the highway to Cambridge taking in the glory of the afternoon while enjoying a whimsical trip to the country. Her fondness for Colin materialized when he invited her home to spend time with his family. They had been dating for a couple of months, and he had been traveling back and forth from Liverpool to London.

She was surprised when one Thursday night Colin casually mentioned, "I'm going home tomorrow. Do you want to come?"

"Sure."

"We'll be staying with my parents. I want you to meet my siblings," he said with a smile. "They can't wait to meet my American girlfriend from the South."

"You talk to them about me?"

"Of course, love," he said. Shirley started packing her things, excited to finally be introduced as a girlfriend. When they arrived, his sister Jules met them at the door.

"Is this Shirley?" Jules inquired.

"Yep, the one and only."

"Come inside, let's take a look," Jules said.

Jules was a petite blonde who wore a lot of blue eye shadow. She spoke with the same clipped Cockney accent as Colin, except she prefaced everything with "darling." His parents' easy manner gave rise to Colin's own demeanor.

"Is this the one you're shagging now?" his mother asked.

"Mum, stop it."

Shirley remained muted. Her folks were not anything like his parents. Colin's parents were liberal about everything. In Shirley's house, it would be unheard of for her to share the same room with a boy she brought home, much less the same bed. When Colin showed them to the room—and bed—they would be sharing, she took it all in stride.

"At least," she thought, "there would be no pretenses here."

At the Carmichael household, Saturday's were designated for chores and Sundays for church. At the Ogelby household, from Friday to Sunday evening, the family started at the pub and went wherever the fancy took them. This weekend, they went to a local soccer match Jules's husband played in and to a barbecue afterward. On Saturday night, Colin suggested a Morrocan restaurant for dinner. Watching Colin get up and goof off with Moroccan dancer, Shirley realized for the first time in their relationship she may have been dealing with a personality she was unprepared for. With Colin up there awkwardly dancing and smiling beckoning her to come join him, she thought, "This one may have been too much for me."

When they settled down for the night, both of them cramped in his twin bed, he said to Shirley, "I'm very glad you came this weekend."

"Me too," she answered.

Shirley looked into his hazel eyes, reached out and touched his face, and then broke rule three. She began to innocently kiss him gently on the mouth. His light licking of her breast only intensified her sudden attraction for him. As he began to descend further south, all Mitzy's admonitions about having sex went out of the window and before she knew it, Shirley was lying on her back with her legs over Colin's shoulders asking herself, "How on Earth did I get like this?"

When it was over, she laid in Colin's arms, promising not to beat herself up over it. The next day her walk of shame was the telltale sign, and Mitzy could only shake her head and say, "You'll learn." Mitzy was a lot kinder than Mave, though.

Mave exclaimed, "You can't do that with men, Shirley, and then expect them to call you back!"

He did. He kept calling her until it was Shirley who, having orders to return to the States, called it off.

"Well, we did have a good run of things," Colin said as he kissed her good-bye at Heathrow.

Chapter Thirty—Moved

Marla did not let the mishap at the altar slow her down. When she moved to Macon, she became a beautician. In her first two years in the city she connected with people who made her forget Hickshaw for a moment. After she earned her license, she began working at Sissy's, an upscale salon. She rented a booth there for $100 a month, which Marla did not mind because she met a wide array of people at the shop.

At twenty, Marla had no idea moving to Macon would burgeon into a whole new life, but four years later she not only managed to build her career but she was also able to secure for herself a reliable social network. She missed her family, but on the occasions when she did return, she was reminded of just how small a place the world could be to someone who no longer belonged to Hickshaw.

Marla was never one to hold personal grudges. In fact, most people found her to be a pleasant person. Oddly though, after the wedding, everyone in Hickshaw grated on Marla's nerves, even when they meant well. Marla no longer bought into the whole idea of being pleasant for pleasant's sake, especially when the people in Hickshaw were not pleasant toward and this attitude permeated Hickshaw.

This new honesty about Hickshaw is why when Mave announced that she, Gus, and the kids would be moving to a new development right outside of Macon, Marla reacted with surprise and uncertainty. Marla knew Mave, and even though Mave's marriage had initially been one of forced compliance, Mave was beginning to become a married woman of Hickshaw in the real sense. Marla began to see Mave with the same look of admonition that appeared on the countenance of the married women in Hickshaw, not so much a frown but a drawing in of the lips that matched a knitting of the brow. Marla noticed it by accident when she was talking to Mave about an earlier trip to Miami while on a visit to Hickshaw.

"We went to a hair show. You would not believe all the amazing products they have available today. They can make your hair stay curled without the curlers," Marla explained.

"Whom'd you go with?" Mave asked.

"Just a few of the stylists from some of the shops in the area."

"Where'd you stay?"

"It was in Miami, but we stayed in North Kendall."

As Marla began to describe the 5,800 square foot home they stayed in, she began to see the creepings of "the look" on Mave's face.

"You know, Marla. You have to be careful around rich folks, especially from the city." Mave continued, "They're a little more sophisticated'n we are." Then Mave's eyes slightly closed and the corners of her mouth tightened.

"We stayed with one of the parents of a stylist in the show. And Mave, they're not wealthy." Marla stopped, looked at Mave, and continued, "Really, they're nice people."

"Isn't it expensive to go to those shows?"

"Part of being good in this business is about travelin' and gettin' new ideas."

Marla did not discuss the show further, but she could not forget that tight, tense look on Mave's face. Marla did not talk about the fascinating boys she met and dated, nor did she talk about some of the eccentric clients who specifically requested she cut their hair. She realized Mave could only handle so much that was different and quite frankly, Marla did not care to be told about how awful a person she was turning into, so she kept that part of her life away from her sister. Conversely, the only change Mave saw in her sister came in the form of avant-garde haircuts and flashy colors paired with the inappropriate clothes and make-up. When Marla learned that Mave and Gus would be moving to town, her response was, "Well, I'm thrilled. We'll be able to spend more time together," all the while knowing and preparing for a barrage of admonitions for the things Marla was, and was not, doing right in her life.

Mave, on the other hand, was unusually excited about the move. The only drawback was the kids would have to change schools. The house Gus and she purchased, with cash, was a split-level three bedroom and three bath settled near a private club house and park. Mave fell in love with the development when she learned it had not only one park but also a second park with a pool. The home had a large kitchen with an island that she immediately began decorating. The Montgomery Ward set she purchased with cash was perfect for the formal living and dining room area. Their first night in their new home, Mave and Gus sat outside watching ducks waddle in a nearby lake. The evening was a warm, humid one, and they both sat entwined in each other's arms.

"Gus, I can't believe we have our own home," she said wistfully.

"It's only gonna get better'n this," he said kissing her on the side of the head. The kids were in bed, and it was the first time the two had been alone together in a while.

"Shirley said when she comes home the next time she'd like to stay with us," Mave said to Gus the day they actually moved into their home.

"It shouldn't be a problem. We gotta guestroom now," Gus said.

"I told ya when I married ya I'd be able to take care of ya."

"And you have," she turned and kissed him on the lips.

Gus seemed nonplussed by the move, but for Mave it had been a big deal. She had desired to leave Hickshaw after so many years. For her, everyone had graduated and left, but eleven years later, she and Gus were still stuck in the routine of Hickshaw. She and Gus were the last to leave, turn the lights off, and close the door. Each year after they graduated, she and Gus watched as another one of their classmates left or graduated from college to go off on some adventure the two of them would never experience. This time it was their turn to cut the ropes that tethered both of them to Hickshaw. After they had decided on a home, she spent most of her days getting to know the surrounding community. She immediately hooked herself and Gus into the Macon Chamber of Commerce, and she went by the local community college, of course. The actual move was not so difficult because by the time the family moved, Mave had been pretty familiar with the area.

Even though they were more than fifty miles from home, Mave made it a promise to attend church every Sunday. She did not want to add to the problem of uprooting her children from the only community they had known. More than anything, she delighted in the fact she and Marla would get to spend more time together. Mave frequently made trips to Macon for lunch and other small outings, and Marla's anxiety about her older sister's judgment of her life soon dissipated because she had found a home away from home. Many weekends Marla stayed the night with Mave, which lent itself to renewing their relationship, and on those rare occasions when Gus and Mave went out of town to spend time alone, Auntie Marla rescued Chet, Lux, and now Charlene into fun-filled weekends of pizza for breakfast and bedtimes after midnight. When Marla did bring a date, the four would go as couples out to Jake's and Jack's Seafood Bistro. One night when Marla spent the night with Mave's family, she and Mave talked about what happened several years before.

"You know, I'm really glad you moved closer," Marla said flatly one day when Mave had not annoyed her.

"Why, because now you have some place to crash?"

"No," Marla chuckled. "Because it's nice to finally be around some family."

"You didn't have to leave."

"I didn't want to stay, especially now with Joe being married."

While no one ever officially told Marla her ex was married, she learned through the grapevine that Joe married someone he met at school shortly after their wedding. Marla did not think of old friends she left behind. She did not think of the fun she had all those summers ago, nor did she think about church gatherings and sitting by the lake in her Sunday wear watching the days pass. In the cloud of all that happiness, Marla could only think of Joe and what he had done to her. Her broken heart was not on display for the world to view, not even years later when she moved on with her life. Joe was her first love, and she held him up in high regard, never belittling any aspect of his personality. Nevertheless, being a seed from the same plant in Hickshaw, Marla knew no matter how she returned to Hickshaw as a successful, independent, and strong woman, she would still be "the one Joe left at the altar." For Marla, that label was not good enough.

"Do you ever want to get married again?" Mave asked while fussing with a flyaway hair on Marla's cheek.

"Mave, I never was married. I got stood up remember? Of course, but I wanna meet the right one this time. I need to trust that person is gonna be open with me about everything."

"Joe and you didn't have that?"

"Honestly speaking, not really. We were kids."

Mave studied her sister for a minute noticing the brassy dyed ringlets that shaped her face.

"Do you sleep with the men you date?" Mave asked, her tone very serious. The question surprised Marla because this was the first time Mave ever asked about her intimacies.

"Sometimes," and she added jokingly, "If they smell good."

Both girls chuckled.

"Does it bother you afterward?" Mave asked.

"No, not really."

"Are you lonely?" Mave asked.

"Sometimes."

Mave studied her sister, who was now in her mid-twenties. She noticed how practically all of the baby fat around her face had transformed into that of a mature woman. Mave more closely resembled her father, but Marla's features were that of her mother, with wide, large eyes separated by a perky nose.

Marla waited for her sister's chastisement but instead she said, "What happened to us, Marla?" while reaching her hand out to touch her little sister's face. "Where did everything go wrong?"

"Just look at them as detours, darlin'." Marla responded, "Life doesn't seem so tough then."

The two of them lay in the double bed in the guest room and were interrupted by Lux, who wanted to know if they could stay up later because Chet was being a tyrant and making them go to bed too early. When Mave left her sister by herself in the bedroom to deal with her children, sadness crept into Marla's soul about what transpired a few years earlier. Between getting her license, developing clientele, and just living single, Marla never considered herself as being lonely. Her life was filled with fabulous friends, but without intimacy, she knew there was emptiness. Marla felt unfulfilled. She moved past Joe, but she was never able to connect and get as comfortable with a man again. As a result, Marla really did not spend too much time getting to really know one man. She assumed because she was single, and the men she dated were single, they must both have uncomfortable histories. The void in her heart had no reservations or promises attached to it for any man.

While Mave attended the children, Marla studied the photos that hung in the guest room, glancing at the furniture and thought to herself, "Even though Mave felt marriage was not good at first, *she made good.*"

Chapter Thirty-one—A Visit

Shirley's next, and final, assignment was MacDill Air Force Base in Tampa. She spent so much time in Europe that she found the cacophony of Southern accents overwhelming. The pale blue waters in the Gulf of Mexico were different from the deep violet of the Mediterranean, the white caps of the Pacific, and the cold choppiness of the Atlantic. In Tampa Bay, she had to go far out into the ocean before leaving the shallow depths. The water was a change from the blue-black water of the other locales with its teal hue.

As a master sergeant, she had more freedom in her living situation and more BHA funds, so she moved into a house off base near the beach. Her first priority was to gain admittance into a graduate program. Her top picks were University of Miami, University of Florida, University of Georgia, and Auburn University, as those were the places where the experts in her field taught. At first, school for Shirley was a whimsical idea. However, by the time she graduated, she earned a degree in engineering for professional reasons. She also was happy to be back stateside because it gave her the opportunity to reconnect with friends and family from home, especially Mave. Her first trip home she did not have time to see or even to talk to Mave. Through the grapevine, she heard that not only had Mave moved but Marla as well. Her first call to Mave after moving stateside kind of surprised her friend.

"Is this the Henriksen residence?" Shirley asked hesitantly.

"Yes, who'd you like to speak with?" answered the adolescent boy.

"Is Mave there?"

"Yes, hold on a minute. Mama! Phone's for you!"

"Well, who is it?"

"I don't know. Some lady," Chet said as he passed the phone to his mother. Shirley heard the shuffling on the other end.

"Hey," Shirley said.

Her voice didn't register to Mave, and then Mave said, "Shirley! Is that you?"

"Yep."

"Where are you? You sound close."

"Mama didn't tell you I was comin' home?"

"Well, no."

"I'm in Florida. I've been stationed here."

"Where?"

"At MacDill in Tampa."

"When are we gonna see you? We bought a new house."

"I know. Mama told me."

"You gotta come see it."

"I know, I know. When is a good time for you?"

"How 'bout this weekend?" Mave said. Even though the trip would be short notice, Shirley really wanted to see her friend, as almost fourteen years passed since she last saw Mave.

When Shirley arrived, everything Mave said about the house was true. It was beautiful and grand, grander than any home Shirley visited.

The first night, she settled into the comfortable guest room Mave set aside for company. Shirley listened to the stillness of the night. She got up and walked out to the door leading to the patio, reclined on the chaise, and watched the tranquility of the pond. Mave heard rustling outside and knocked on Shirley's door to find she was outside. She opened the screen door to see Shirley lounging.

"Hey, sleepy head," Mave said. Shirley turned to Mave.

"Hey," Shirley said and then Mave sat on the edge of the lounger. Shirley watched the water and then she said, "What's on tap for tomorrow?"

"Well, I thought we'd get gussied up at Marla's, and then Gus and I are gonna take you t'dinner," Mave said.

"Sounds good," Shirley said. The two women sat in the morning air and talked about old times for about two hours when Mave got up from the lounger.

"Don't spend too much time out here. It gets chilly," Mave said.

Soon after Mave went back into the house, Shirley followed. The next day, they started out early to downtown Macon. At the salon turned spa, Shirley had the works. She cut off the waist long hair that weighed her face down for almost a decade and a half and turned it into a manageable bob. She had her first pedicure and manicure, in addition to waxing her unibrow. Marla suggested she stick to light make-up like pinks and reds for lipstick because she was a summer.

By the time the two girls walked out of the place, it was almost three. Gus told Mave the reservations were for five, so they immediately showered and changed. Mave put on a simple black dress that accentuated her now very curvaceous body while Shirley wore a pantsuit and strappy sandals. Shirley had so enjoyed hanging out with Mave Saturday that when Mave announced incidentally that Charlie Munswinger, Gus's contracting buddy, would be joining them for dinner, Shirley grew slightly annoyed.

"What time did Charlie say he'd meet us?" Mave asked Gus nonchalantly, as she checked her lipstick in the passenger's side mirror.

"A little after five. He's got some meetin', so he said he'd be a little shy of five," he paused, and then turned toward Mave. "I thought we could have a drink while we waited," Gus said, looking in the rearview mirror at Shirley.

Before she could answer, Mave turned around in her seat to Shirley and said, "You're gonna like Charlie. He's real cute, has no children, and has only been divorced once."

"They're separated, Mave" Gus interjected.

Mave looked at Gus. "She's been gone for three years. She's not comin' back." Mave shot back and then continued, "His family's loaded." She smiled an encouraging grin to which Shirley returned the same version of the smile back to Mave. Inside, though, Shirley seethed. Mave never mentioned Charlie or her double dating with Charlie the whole time while they were at the salon. Shirley did not know whether to feel offended or not, but she sure was annoyed. Mave did not see any harm in it because she set up Marla with a few of Gus's nice business friends and it had not been a problem with Marla. Shirley told Mave about her plans for school and all the traveling she had done in Europe, never mentioning desires to date or be married. To Mave, though, Shirley could have been elected president, and it would not have mattered much if she did not have a man to go along with the White House.

When they arrived at the club, Charlie was indeed everything Mave had said he was, except he was still married. He was probably the perfect person for Shirley, except she did not want him either. Shirley remained her usual quiet, cordial self and let Mave do most of the talking over dinner. Mave gushed about the places Shirley visited and lived, and Shirley sat quietly making a few comments here and there, still annoyed at her friend's presumption. As Mave conversed, Shirley studied Mave, watching the red-lacquered nails clink against the cocktail glass as Mave finished off the last few drops of Southern Comfort.

Something in Mave had changed, and Shirley did not know what. Gone was the happy, young woman who really did not measure her worth against what others had, and in place was this person who had become an extension of her life, her wealth, her husband. This feeling Shirley had was only solidified later when the evening ended and she finished saying good-bye to Charlie. Shirley overheard the tail end of the conversation Gus had with Mave, who both, by this time, were standing by their truck politely arguing.

"You should've told her Mave." Gus continued, "She may not even wanna date, having had her heart broken by that boy in Japan."

"That was years ago and she's had others since then," Mave said.

"Still, you shoulda told her. You really shouldn't interfere in people's personal affairs. We talked about that," Gus said.

"They're gettin' along fine. Look," she said pointing to Shirley and Charlie, both standing by Charlie's vehicle and saying their good-byes.

When Mave realized Shirley was approaching, she turned to her. "Hey, sweetheart, are you ready to call it a night?"

"Yeah, I'm kinda beat."

In the car, Mave asked, "So how'd you like him?"

"He's a nice sorta fella. Where did you find him?"

Ignoring Shirley's snarky remark, Mave prattled on about how Gus connected with Charlie through business. Even though things had changed for Shirley, they were still the same for Mave.

The next morning Shirley joined Mave, Gus, and the kids in their

Sunday trek to town for church. The day was a muggy one, and Shirley just watched as the ladies in the pews used the programs to fan the stifling heat from around them. After leaving her friend, she joined her family for a late lunch and started on her journey back to Florida. Driving to Tampa, the early morning blackness provided stillness to her thoughts of loneliness and regret.

At first Shirley was hurt by Mave's actions. While innocent, Mave's behavior made her friend feel as if she was no longer valued, much less valuable. She wondered, as she drove the small red clay road out of town, whether that decision she made all those years ago was a punishment for the loneliness she was currently feeling. With no boyfriend and no prospects, it was like God was telling her, "I gave you a man, but you didn't want him." She was being punished, even though she tried to avoid an unhappy, passionless marriage because she did not even feel the kind of emotions for Duck that a wife should. In the cool breeze, she reflected on her solitude and drove home in the blackness of the night.

Chapter Thirty-two—Steppin' Out

"Wanna go to a hair show?" Marla asked.

"A hair show?" Mave clarified, scrunching up her nose at Marla.

"Yeah, it's in Atlanta," Marla said, prodding her sister on. "Oh, come on. You never have been to one. It'll be fun."

"Let me talk to Gus. See if he's doin' anything this weekend and get back to you."

Mave had been around Marla's friends and she liked them, but they were of a different sort. She liked her friendships tame, and while she had heard the shop talk frequently, she did not know if she could stand a weekend of the bawdy, coarse group. Marla thought it would be a good idea to invite her sister only because Mave, while only in her early thirties, took on mannerisms of a woman much older. Marla really had not paid attention to Mave until one weekend when Marla happened to visit and was surrounded by a few old friends from Hickshaw who were sitting outside on the patio enjoying the midday breeze and playing pinochle.

"Anyone need a refill on their beverages?" Marla asked.

"No," the girls chimed in unison. Then Mave piped in, "Hold on," and she drank the last contents of the glass, including the ice cubes, and handed her sister the glass emptied of its contents. Mave must have sucked on those cubes for what seemed like forever. Marla was not bothered by her sucking on the ice, but it was the way she sucked on the ice, sliding it slowly from one side of her mouth to the other until it melted, reminding Marla, actually, of her mother. "Lord, Mave," she thought to herself, "You're too young to be gettin' old." To Marla's surprise, Mave agreed to go to the hair show. Watching her little sister participate in her profession, Mave had a sudden newfound respect for Marla.

After the night of the show, the girls found themselves in the Bar Shark, an establishment frequented by down-home folks from Atlanta. Mave, Marla, and some of the other stylist had been enjoying a cocktail when Mave noticed out of the corner of her eye a blond's gaze. Marla noticed too, and when the man approached both of them at the bar, Mave lowered her eyes in feigned nonchalance.

"Would you like to dance?" he asked Mave.

"Sure," Mave said and slid off her barstool into the arms of the aforementioned partner.

Her partner's touch felt weird to Mave. The only other person that she held this closely in her entire life was Gus. She looked into her partner's eyes, and the chemistry was frighteningly staticky. She held his stare, and for the first time since she married, her heart fluttered and she felt a tingling down south. When he pulled her closer to him, she could smell the strong scent of Brut cologne. Blushing beet red by now, Mave held his gaze, not even noticing his hand sliding into the pockets of her back jean pocket and cupping her bottom. The two must have been looking pretty intimate because Marla placed her long island iced tea on the bar and marched out on the dance floor.

"Mave, honey, can I speak to you for a minute?"

"Yes," Mave said, excusing herself from her partner.

"What are you doin'?" Marla asked.

"I'm just dancin', Marla," Mave said. "It's innocent." She explained apologetically, not wanting to spoil their weekend together.

Marla said, "Well we're about t'go."

"Okay, well let me say good-bye to—" and Mave looked around to see the fella had gone. She laughed and followed Marla out of the club. The ride home the next day Mave was quiet.

"What's on your mind?" Marla asked.

"Oh, nothin'," Mave said absentmindedly and continued to stare out the window.

"Look, I know you've not been happy, Mave, and for a long time. If ya think cheatin' is gonna solve your problems—"

"What do ya mean?" Mave asked and continued, "Marla, it's been so long since I've felt free—just to be able to have someone look at me with such—" Mave trailed off.

"Desire?" Marla finished.

"Well, yeah, desire."

"Girl, that was lust," Marla said flatly and the two laughed.

"Okay, well lust."

Marla stopped talking. Marla wanted tell Mave she would eventually be free in couple of years to live the way she wanted, but she did not want to encourage her sister to leave her marriage.

Instead Marla said, "Being alone is not for the faint of heart Mave. It's been so long since I even remember what it felt like to be intimate with someone. You should talk to Mama."

Even though her mother had been married almost forty years, Mave did not want to even broach the topic. Mama was a very cut-and-dry woman. If a woman married, she stayed married, no matter the consequence. Her mother would be of little real help in this situation. For this reason, Mave talked to Marla hoping that she would give Mave permission to be free in her marriage.

"That man was not just lookin' at me with lust. I really felt a connection," Mave said.

Marla said, "Mave, dear, you may be older'n me and know a lot more about raisin' a family, but in this I know that man you were dancin' with probably handled any number of women in the same manner last night."

"And how'd do you know?"

"In another time, I probably would have been one of those women," she joked. "But seriously, Mave honey, that's not what yer lookin' for."

They drove in silence and when Marla stopped the car to let Mave out, Marla said, "Forgive yourself." Mave stepped out the car and shut the door to go to her own life.

On her drive home, Mave thought about the dance the night before. She had not felt that way since high school. The excitement of having someone look at her and touch her in a truly sexual way had long since passed. The rapidly beating heartbeat and hushed breath reminiscent of high school rendezvous by the lake was a distant memory to the quick and hurried moments of love shared between her and Gus in their fifteen years of marriage. She felt guilty because never once had she considered cheating, but the rush of feeling like that seventeen-year-old kid in the backseat of a car stealing kisses was like gold. When she returned to Gus, she slightly pecked him on the cheek.

"How was the hair show?" Gus asked.

"Like bein' at a fashion show for hair," Mave said while quickly heading to the bedroom.

"Oh well, Charlene's got an open house. She came home Friday with a note."

"What time?"

"Six o'clock."

Mave fell right back into the routine of her life. She did, however, pause to wonder about the excitement in their marriage. Not that they were overly intimate, but early in the marriage their coupling had left a lasting effect on her enough for her to want to stay. The intensity of the love Gus felt for her was shown during these times. In this time, they had frustrated sex, both trying to scratch an itch while doing it quickly so neither one of their brood would interrupt them. She wanted to tell him what she needed, but she could not because either he would think he was not doing enough or that she had found a better partner. She said nothing, and when he was finished, she remembered a time when his lovemaking fulfilled every need she had.

Mave never once had to worry about Gus's faithlessness to her or his commitment to marriage, and even now she was confident that he never was unfaithful to her. Had it not been for Marla, Mave may have carried the dancing further than she would have been able to forgive herself, even to the point of her being comfortable enough with him having an affair if he desired, and this fact bothered her. Mave just needed someone to free her from the shackles of her own life.

Chapter Thirty-three—Consequences

H ey, Wilkerson," Jamie's commanding office said.

After he saluted the officer, Jamie said, "Yes, sir."

"Come into my office for a second. Your orders have come in," Sergeant Okes said.

"Where to next?" Jamie asked as the sergeant handed Jamie the envelope. Jamie opened the envelope and looked at the contents and said, "I see Ramstein is on the list again."

Jamie and Francesca spent four years at Ramstein and both enjoyed the diversions that this particular assignment offered.

Before Jamie could say anything, the commanding officer said, "Jamie," and then his supervisor got up to close the door. "Jamie, you might not want Ramstein this time."

Jamie looked behind him to see his supervisor return to his desk.

"Look, Wilkerson, I don't listen to office scuttlebutt, but you and your wife, you and Francesca. Well, there's been talk."

"Talk of what?"

"Well, okay, apparently, you and your wife, on numerous occasions, have frequented the District in Amsterdam."

"What?" Then Jamie exclaimed, "Me and my wife are faithful to each other."

The sergeant put his hands in front of him in a somewhat defensive posture.

"Jamie, I'm not judging you. I'm telling you this because I don't want you to get thrown out of the military, especially for conduct that could easily be corrected."

Jamie sat in the chair, quite sullen because he was sure that no one knew of that one occurrence that happened a few years earlier.

Jamie then said, "I don't know what to say, but it's completely and utterly not true."

The sergeant said, still persistent that he had in fact been told the truth, "I know you are a good person. I just thought you and Francesca might want a new start, go someplace different."

Jamie did not say anything because what his sergeant said was not necessarily true nor was it a lie, and while Jamie was not the most transparent person, he was not a liar.

"Let me see," Jamie said, looking at the list.

"Take it home, Jamie. You have a few weeks before you need to make a decision," the sergeant said.

At home, Jamie did not really say anything to his wife when she returned from the club.

"Look what I brought you," Francesca said, holding the Styrofoam box out toward him.

"What is it?"

"Smothered chicken. I know it's your favorite," she said.

Jamie took the box from her. "Is it all for me?"

"Yep, I ate earlier," Francesca said while walking to the back of the unit. Since leaving Italy, Jamie and Francesca stopped eating at the table together. Jamie sat in front of the television and ate supper. A few minutes later, Francesca joined him in the living room.

Still stinging from the conversation he had with Sergeant Okes, Jamie said, "You know what my supe told me today?"

"No," Francesca said while sipping on her Tab.

"We were seen frequenting brothels in Amsterdam," Jamie said in a flat tone.

Francesca laughed and then covered her mouth. This reaction from Francesca was quite common, and one that Jamie would normally find endearing, cute, but in this moment, he found this reaction extremely annoying.

"Do you not take anything seriously?" he asked Francesca while placing the Styrofoam box on the coffee table.

"What do you mean by that?" she asked.

"Francesca, do you understand that dalliance we had in Amsterdam nearly two years ago has turned into us now frequenting brothels?"

"Who cares? I don't care what these military wives have to say about me, about us," Francesca said.

"They weren't women. My commanding officer told me this, and what that means is that whatever we did was bad enough for someone on that trip that they reported it to someone in my chain of command for them to say something to me about it. You may not care, but I do," Jamie said, and this time he looked at her, trying to understand why he married her.

"I'm not saying it's not important."

"Good, because it is important. It's important that you know we can't just do whatever we want. There are rules."

"Jamie, don't lecture me about rules. I'm in this military as well,"

Francesca said and then asked, "Anyway, where are we moving?"

"Where?"

"We're going back to Italy."

Jamie had also been given the opportunity to move to other bases, including one that was stateside, but he decided Aviano might be better for both him and Francesca.

Chapter Thirty-four—Bruce

Gus grew into the type of man any wife would want. He loved his wife and his children with all the heart a man could. Even in the early years when he knew Mave did not want to be married, it was painful for him but he stayed. Whereas Gus saw the wedding band on his finger as a symbol of their freedom to be with each other as intimately and as passionately as they wanted, Mave saw the band as a chain that imprisoned her to him. The only reason he stayed married was because he listened to the counsel of those who had walked that road before him.

"Son, things'll settle after five or six years," his father advised him.

"Ya sure?"

"Yep. The first couple of years after you get use'ta each other are kinda rocky. Then it just seems like you become one."

"I dunno. Sometimes when I catch her, it's like she's lookin' at me like I stole somethin' from her," Gus said.

His father laughed and said, "Wait it out. You were young and didn't have the opportunity to really understand this marriage thing. Just wait it out. Mave's not goin' anywhere."

This advice, in addition to his father-in-law's pearls of wisdom, was the glue that kept him in the marriage, even when he suspected

Mave had an eye for other men. They had been together for almost fifteen years when his whole picture of their family fractured almost permanently.

Mave was off with Marla picking out a new outfit she wanted to wear out with Davis Morrison, Marla's newest steady. Gus was on his way out the door to pick up some tiles for a contract he was beginning that day. Looking for his cap, he walked into the laundry room to see it sitting right next to the laundry bin in the washroom. As he reached for it, a tiny slip of bright yellow construction paper caught his attention. The paper was torn so he could not see the image in the ad, but it looked like a flyer for a party. Written in very large handwriting, the torn slip of paper said, "Bruce. 415-8277."

He just folded the piece of paper and put it in the outside garbage can. The whole day he could hardly concentrate for thoughts of Mave doing what he had always feared and expected. Not being the violent, cussing type, he just thought about Mave, the life they built, and the friends they made. In those few minutes, his entire life became a lie. When she returned later that evening, he watched her and wondered to himself, "Was it really worth it loving someone whose sole reason for being married was to escape shame?"

Gus never said a word to Mave about his discovery. He just listened as Mave chattered on about Marla's new man and swallowed hard on each spoonful of chili. When she collapsed next to Gus on the sofa while they watched a rerun of Chips, his arms loosely fell around her neck and he wondered how she could not tell his heart was breaking before her. At bedtime, he kissed her good night almost like he would a child, lightly pecking her forehead, reaching for the lamp, and shutting off the light. Mave never noticed the change in his behavior.

Never being overly affectionate, the two resumed their lives as a married couple, in sync with each other's physical needs, but Gus checked out emotionally. He was not angry or bitter toward Mave.

However, in the place where his passion for his wife existed, his passion for his children took root. He often skipped work to chaperone a field trip for Lux or Charlene. As Chet had yet to graduate, he spent a lot of the time he had with the boy. While Gus's life had not been a total disaster, he wanted to make sure Chet did not walk in the footsteps of his father, as he did not want Chet to make the same mistakes. Gus knew Chet was not interested in college, so summers when he was out of school, he arranged for the boy to work alongside him as Gus's own father had done previously for him, but he spoke to him the way parents do when they fear their own failings being repeated in their children.

With Mave, he soon developed a passive resistance, viewing her like he did Chet, Lux, or Charlene. One evening, as she applied lipstick perfectly to her face before they went out, Gus envisioned a child standing before her mirror in her mother's oversized shoes playing in make-up. He actually had to catch himself because he laughed out loud.

"What's so funny?" Mave returned a playful giggle.

"Oh, nothing. Are you gonna put some rouge on?" he asked and continued to watch his child-wife put herself together. She came over to playfully kiss him, and he politely grabbed her hands and said, "Aw, come on Mave. You're gonna get that stuff all over me. Plus, we don't have time."

The marriage flowed in this way. Sometimes Gus could avoid the more intimate duties of the marriage with discussions about building a life together, family, hopes for their children, and so forth. Other times, when Mave's advances could not be muted, he put himself through the paces, closing off that part of him that was devoted to the girl he thought the world of at one time. The crudely piece of ultraviolet yellow advertising long since discarded, he never once said a word to his wife about how it broke him to his core.

186

Chapter Thirty-five—A Married Woman's Nightmare

Charlene was Mave's third, and final, child. In this moment, family and friends would gather for the girl's seventh birthday.

"Okay, Charlene, go ahead and blow those candles out. Come on now, girl, you have to blow really hard," Mave said, encouraging her youngest daughter.

"And try not to spit on the cake this time," Lux said.

"Oh, shut up, Lux," Chet said and moved closer to Charlene to take a picture. He continued, "Now, Charlene, say cheese!"

"Chet, don't stand too close. You won't get Charlene in the picture," Mave said.

Born in the middle of winter, Charlene was not happy that her birthday was at the end of a harsh winter freeze, which also meant that the gas heater had to be reset every four hours so as not to overheat and melt down the heater.

"All right guys, I gotta go reset the heater. Make sure that ya don't give Charlene too much of that cake. I don't want her up all night," Mave said. "Come on, Josie. I need someone to hold the flashlight. It's dark down there." Mave and Josie walked down to the basement where the electric heater sat.

"Mave, did you really need to reset that heater?" Josie asked.

"No, can you believe that Macey showed up?" Mave said with a feigned disgusted voice as she got ready to discuss the latest town tidbit about the newest divorcee.

"Yes, Mave, she's gotta a daughter that happens to be one of Charlene's favorite friends."

"I mean, I know I invited her, but with the divorce an' all, I thought they woulda rather stay home. I mean, I would've," Mave said.

"I kinda feel bad for her," Josie said.

"But why? Usually it's somethin' the woman's done. Coreen talked to her just right after it happened. Macey said he'd been seein' that gal for a while."

"God, that's terrible. I mean ta'think that you have a good marriage, and then some woman comes along and caput. Yer marriage is gone."

"I don't know. Don't care. I just want her to take her little Chrissy—"

"Her name is Christy, Mave," Josie said.

"Okay, Christy, and take her and get outta here before whatever she has catches onto all of us and we're all divorced," Mave said.

"Okay, okay, okay, Mave. Get a hold of yourself. Macey is someone we've been friends with. Her getting divorce has no bearing on our lives," Josie said.

"Oh yeah? What about the Hendersons and their divorce. Judy use'ta be over there all the time and now her and Hank are splittin' up. Call me superstitious but divorce is catching in Hickshaw, and I refuse to be a casuality," Mave said.

"Oh, all right Mave, but please, at least be civil. Your daughter associates with this child in school," Josie said.

Mave put her hands up in the air and said, "All right! All right."

"Let's go get us some cake," Josie said leading the way. The two women walked up the short flights of stairs only to be joined by Coreen.

Coreen asked, "What were you doin' down there?"

Mave said, "Fixin' the heat."

"Yeah right. I wanna know what you told her," Coreen said in Josie's direction.

"Oh, come on," Josie said, "This is worse'n high school."

"Just say it quickly," Coreen said.

"You already know. He's seein' somebody," Josie said.

"Oh that. Come on, let's get back to the party," Coreen said.

Just before Charlene finished the last bite of cake, Mave found the kindness to go over to Macey and offer her some cake and words of support and advice. Then she decided to stay away from the dreadful woman the rest of the afternoon.

Chapter Thirty-six—Odd Man Out

L ooking around it appeared to be an ordinary day, but for the Henriksens, it was their fifteenth anniversary. Mave noticed the change. Last year, and practically every year when they could afford it, Gus made sure the kids had a babysitter, and she and her husband would find time to rediscover each other during a short vacation Gus planned. Mave was oblivious to the turmoil stirring in her husband, but she pushed the slip to the back of her mind.

On another day, though, Mave became aware of the slight shift that transformed their relationship and, more importantly, her relationship to her kids. She drove into Macon to get "the works." All polished up, she returned to her family, who had just come home from an afternoon with their father. Normally Gus spent time with the kids on the weekend, but Mave noticed that lately he had been spending an inordinate amount of time with them. She walked in, and the family was in the middle of eating burgers their father grilled. The three kids sat at the table in the kitchen and Gus ate at the island. All four had mouths full of hamburger and were laughing so loudly she heard the laughter before she opened the door.

"Hey," Mave said. "What'd your daddy cook?"

"Burgers," Charlene answered.

"Smells good," Mave said.

Usually seeing their mother was home, one of the kids would move from the table to the island and let Mave have a seat. No one moved. She waited a minute, and still all three sat engaged in their conversation. Gus also noticed the slight but was too preoccupied with fixing his plate to correct the children.

"Chet, move so your mama can sit down," Gus said to his son.

Chet looked at his father and then slowly he peeled himself out of the chair, carried his plate, and moved toward the island. Mave fixed a plate and helped herself to some of the chips in the bag. As soon as Chet moved, the girls picked up their plates and joined their father and brother at the island. Mave watched the two girls toddle off to join the others.

"What, do I smell bad or somethin'?" she asked, trying to get them to laugh. Everyone laughed and then continued to eat. Mave knew she had abandoned them for the day, so she was trying to make up for it with humor.

"So, what did ya'll do today?" Mave asked Gus.

"Took the kids shopping, a movie. Nothin' much," Gus said.

"What did ya'll see?

"Star Wars," Chet answered as he picked his plate up, washed it, and put it in the dishwasher.

"How's Auntie Marla?" Lux asked.

"She's fine. She wants to know if yer gonna need your hair done for Spring Cotillion."

"Probably not. I'll just curl it myself."

"Well, if you change your mind you gotta' let her know soon. It's that season and they're startin' to book quickly."

More silence and then Chet broke in, "Daddy, ya think Fox could come along with us to Bear Brook next weekend?" Bear Brook was not actually a brook but more like a river. However, it was one of the best places to visit during the early spring.

"Sure, I don't see why not," Gus answered.

"Gus, did ya forget that we have plans over at the Hansons?" Mave said plainly and stopped chewing. Chet looked at his mother with concern that his plans may be interrupted, but he remained quiet and let his father talk.

"You can go, Mave. I already made the reservations and promised the boy I'd take him."

"But Gus, I can't believe you," she said.

Gus told the kids, now all finished eating, to go to their rooms and get ready for bed. Then the arguing ensued. After the first five minutes, the Henriksens no longer battled about the boy's trip, but the argument covered a range of topics like Mave's late hours and Gus's over indulgent attitude toward the kids. In the comfort of Chet's room, where the three children usually congregated when their parents fought, they listened to their mother and father contend with each other, quite loudly, about everything big and small that had gone wrong in their marriage.

The sting of the evening's slight was felt the next morning when the two of them, Mave sitting on the couch and Gus on the loveseat, apologized to each other for their behavior the previous night. Mave was not mad about Bear Brook, nor was she mad about the fight, but the hurt came when each one of her children awoke, ate breakfast, and joined their father on the small loveseat one by one while Mave took up a little portion of the large sofa. She was bewildered. Even so, she watched television with her family, quietly upset but processing the change. After a little while, Gus told the kids to go finish their chores, and when they finished, they would visit their grandparents later.

"I thought it might be nice if we went to the park," Mave said.

Gus looked at his children, the mirror reflection of his image, and said, "Well, it's up to ya'll."

"Didn't you tell Grandma we'd be comin'?" Chet asked.

"Yes," but before Gus could finish Mave said, "Well fine, I suppose there are a million things I could do 'round here."

"Why don't you come?" asked Lux.

"No, you go on. Spend some time with your grandparents."

Mave left the sofa and went to the office where she paid the household bills and listened for their departure while her heart broke. The only indication they had left was the click of the lock on the door.

Gus drove while listening to his brood cajole in the truck. In deep thought, he was carried to another time.

He and Mave were celebrating their previous anniversary. The thought of the intimacy they shared filled him with such love that he hardly remembered Bruce. They spent a week at Lake Havasu, and it was like they were back in high school sitting in the inner tubes on Lake White while the sun shun. The highlights in her hair spun a brilliant gold almost hypnotizing him.

"I wish we could be like this forever," he said.

"Yes, life is good," Mave answered.

Times like this made Mave glad they were married. For Gus, his love had grown into a patient one as he waited for his wife to mature. She was not outright neglectful, but she would just close off, leaving Gus and her children out of her world. Not being able to attend school was a disappointment for her. He knew it, but he tried to make up for her sacrifice by being a good provider, being faithful, and being a good father. In some ways, she let him know the life he gave her was disappointing. When she started volunteering, she obviously was fed up with being a homemaker. He thought, though, when they got married, their marriage would be a joint effort. The first couple of years, he ignored the little slights, but he could not ignore her neglect of his children.

The worst instance was when she wanted to go from being a volunteer to being a part-time librarian. When the kids were at school, she would work for four hours and be home in time to meet the kids and make dinner. During this time, she heard about a full-time position in the library that was going to open up. The head librarian said the job was hers if she wanted it, but she would have to work full-time and work toward her degree. Without consulting Gus, she said she could take the job, but the availability date she needed to discuss with Gus. After work, she went straight to the junior college and enrolled in two classes for the next term. The elation she felt as she tucked her schedule in her purse was a new and rare feeling, having left that girl who experienced that kind of joy at the altar. That feeling was temporary because, as she drove into the subdivision, she realized she forgot her daughter at school. Little Charlene sat on the stoop, backpack and lunch pail in front of her.

"I'm sorry, Mama got held up today," Mave said.

"I've only been waiting a few minutes," Charlene said, following her mother into the house. Charlene was a lot kinder than Gus when he discovered the slip. Everyone was at the dinner table eating, and Charlene, Lux, and Chet talked about school.

"Yeah, while I was waiting on Mama, I saw Gracie's cat. She's gonna have a litter," Charlene said.

"The calico?" Lux asked.

"Why were you late?" Gus interjected.

"I had to go by the school to enroll in some courses," Mave said

194

while continuing to listen to the children.

"Ah, Mave, we're not gonna go over this again," Gus said in absolute frustration and then threw his napkin on the table.

"For me to have this job, I havta enroll in courses."

"Mave, you got a job?" He asked, his voice slightly elevated.

"Yes, there is an openin' at the library and they offered it to me. I'm gonna take it."

"What about the kids?"

"We'll give the kids a key. They'll be fine," she said, trying to pacify Gus.

Everyone sat quietly at the table. Mave was going to tell him later when the kids were sleeping. However, this conversation would not wait. The conversation began in the usual tone husbands and wives use when they are about to discuss something important, but then it took a turn for the worse.

"You don't havta work, Mave. We talked 'bout this already."

Something rose up in Mave because she threw her napkin on the table, got up from the table, and said, while gesturing with her hands out in front of her, "Gus, this is not enough for me anymore." She then left her family at the table.

"You kids clean up. Me and your mama need to talk," Gus said to the kids while looking at his wife. Gus followed Mave into the bedroom.

Mave stood her ground until the next morning when she told Mrs. Mills, "I'm sorry I told you I could take the job, but my family commitments won't permit me to work."

Gus reflected on that argument and on Bruce. He then turned the radio up in the car to drown out the sound of his jubilant children.

Chapter Thirty-seven—An Epiphany

I think it's time we had children," Jamie said.

"What do you mean, Jamie?"

"It's time, Francesca. I think we're ready," he said while nuzzling the side of her neck.

"I don't know, Jamie. Raising children takes a lot of work and we've been by ourselves for so long."

"I'm ready," he said.

Francesca did not protect herself this time. Normally she would use diaphragm, but this evening she did not use anything. In this moment, though, she and Jamie were making love, and Francesca was trying to find a way to avoid motherhood. She would get through this moment, pray that she did not come up pregnant, and from this point on, she would just use the pills to avoid Jamie's questions.

Francesca did not really want children. Because her parents were always at the restaurant, she spent most of her time taking care of her younger brothers and sisters. She found children very time consuming with very little, or no, rewards. Jamie did not know about her desire not to be a mother until about six months after their wedding. This news did not bother him because, at the time, he was not quite ready to have children himself. He felt Francesca would get over any fears she might have concerning motherhood.

After the move back to Aviano, the couple went back and forth between him asking her for children and her trying to avoid the whole topic altogether. Upon returning to Aviano, one of the promises Francesca made to Jamie was to really try to become a wife in the real way. For Jamie, being a real wife meant having children, but for Francesca, becoming a real wife meant being more attentive to his needs. The only problem was Francesca did not understand his need to have children, which only increased the longer they stayed together.

Jamie would not understand Francesca's commitment to avoiding parenthood until they had to go to a christening for one of the nephews. Jamie, while putting on aftershave, nicked himself as he shaved. Looking for a tiny piece of gauze in the bathroom cabinet, Jamie could not find any. He then looked in the cupboard under the sink. Not quite out in the open, Jamie looked into Francesca's little variety case to find her birth control pills. As had become customary in their marriage, Jamie would put away the offending piece of information he found—in this case, the pills—and put his anger to the back of his mind in order to not arouse any anger in Francesca at him invading her privacy. More importantly, he never mentioned it to his wife.

"Jamie, hurry up! Katia's going to be mad if we show up late at the church," Francesca said from the front of the small villa they rented.

Both of them rode in Jamie's Mini Cooper, each keeping their own separate thoughts to themselves. At the church, Jamie sat next to Francesca while listening to the priest say rites over the child. He watched the small bundle fidget as the priest sprinkled holy water on the child, and he wondered what it might be like to hold a child, a child of his own.

Francesca placed her hand on his and played with Jamie's index and middle fingers. He looked at her and gave her the most sardonic grin. He did not know what to think of his earlier discovery, so he did not think anything for the rest of the ceremony. The family gathered at the restaurant after the ceremony, and Jamie listened to the family tell the same stories they had in the years they had married. This time the retelling was different. The folktales took on a surreal bend when he began to look around the restaurant to see the children of his in-laws playing, cajoling, and laughing as the parents regaled each other of tales of earlier times. The room became hot and stuffy, so much so that Jamie had to go out to the patio to get some air.

"Jamie. Jamie," Francesca called from him. "Are you all right?" she asked.

He answered, "Yeah, I just needed a little air."

"We could go home. I know you must be tired. I didn't think about you having to work for so long last night." Francesca was right. Jamie was tired from a ten-hour shift he had to pull when the base went on alert.

"No, Francesca. We just got here."

"Something's wrong, Jamie."

"Nothing's wrong, Come on. Let's go back inside," Jamie said. He stopped watching the children, and by evenings end whatever anger he had toward his wife had dissipated.

When he made love to her that evening he asked her, "Did you remember to take your pills?"

Francesca said, "Yes." Then she made to love him.

Chapter Thirty-eight—Better to Have Loved

Gus loved Mave but would rather leave her than see her harm his children. His wife and eldest daughter were very close. Of the three children, Lux seemed to be the glue that held Mave to family life. At first, he had not paid attention to it, but around Lux's sixteenth birthday he saw Mave's attitude toward his second daughter change. Lux and Mave were planning Lux's sixteenth birthday party for a while—who to invite, who to exclude—when memories of Mave's own blossoming took her to a time when she herself was innocent, young, and still getting a sense of her own importance in the community.

Lux and her mother had just ordered the cake from the local Piggly Wiggly when in a moment of excitement Lux suggested, "Mama, we should go shopping for matching outfits."

"Lux, aren't you a little old for that? Why, we haven't done that in a while."

"Oh, come on, Mama. I'll only be sixteen once," Lux said. Mave did not see any harm in it, as she and her daughter often wore the same outfits. When they both stepped out into the living room and started dancing in the middle of the room with a few of Lux's friends, Gus did not find the sight of his wife parading around in a matching halter top and jean set too comforting. Before Mave got too much more into the moment, Gus pulled her aside.

"Go change," he said abruptly to his wife while Lux's friends trickled in for her Sweet Sixteen birthday party.

"What?" Mave asked. She did not see anything wrong with the Jordache jeans and halter top set she purchased for Lux and her for the party that night, but Gus found it to be inappropriate and distasteful on this particular this night.

"Go change your clothes. This is Lux's night. She doesn't need her mama paradin' around in the same outfit," Gus said while looking over Mave's head at his teenage daughter who was enjoying herself. Mave told Lux she would return to the party and went to change. She and Gus never spoke a word about the conversation the entire evening.

"Mama, why'd you go change?" Charlene asked later when Mave returned to the party.

"It's Lux's party. She should be the only one dressed up."

Then there was the time Lux was offered a seat in a summer culinary internship program at the University of Georgia. When the acceptance letter came in the mail, Mave smiled and said, "Good for you, honey." At dinner that night, her brother and sister congratulated her on her achievement. Her father kissed her on the forehead and said, "I'm happy for you, baby."

Mave watched it all and said, "You know yer gonna need to bring those grades up."

"Mama, I've already been accepted," Lux said. The young woman did not know how to take this last comment because usually her mother was very supportive of her efforts regardless of the impact on her grades.

"Books first, young lady," Mave said.

However, Gus knew. He knew what this admonition was really

about and added, "We'll go shoppin' for the things you'll need this weekend. As far as I'm concerned, yer goin'." Mave glared at him, the anger seething underneath the surface of her words.

"Fine honey, you and Daddy go shoppin'."

The final straw came about a month later. Lux's body was filling out. The washboard stomach and boyish hips were beginning to develop into a shapely, younger version of Mave. Lux looked like her daddy, but she had the figure of her mama. Her sandy, blonde ringlets shaped the petite face. Lux was on her way out the door on a date when Mave stopped her. Giving her the once over, Mave's gaze seemed stuck on the little bit of hip that caressed the eyes.

"Those jeans are too tight," Mave said, phrased as a command instead of a comment.

"I'm not changin'. My date's in the car," Lux said.

"He'll have to wait. Go take'm off or yer not goin' anywhere," Mave said with her hand on her hips. Lux ran back to the bedroom, changed her pants, and flew out the door, slamming it without saying good-bye to anyone.

"What did you say to her?" Gus asked.

"Gus, I just told her she had to change. Those jeans were too tight!" Mave added, "These girls like to wear their jeans so tight it leaves nothin' to the imagination."

Gus let it go, but he also knew it was time for him to leave with his children. He could not run interference for his children all the time, and with the other fidelity issues he never addressed with Mave, he did not trust their care to her. Gus was beginning to understand that staying married to Mave was not the best solution presently. He felt guilty for taking her opportunity for an education away from her. He knew not being able to attend college really set her back emotionally, and the sacrifice she was forced to make bothered him. To him, in her mind, he had held her back.

Marriage had not been easy for Gus either. While he loved Mave, ever so often he was reminded of the mistake he made so his children would be safe. On the ride home from work one evening, he remembered the one time he was unfaithful in thought. Chet had just been born, and the reality of being father hit him. Gus was not used to being made responsible for others, and he felt overwhelmed. After work, he met a high school buddy for a drink. He sat in Tilt, a local watering hole, with one of his high school buddies, Ajax. Ajax was given this moniker after a practical joke he played on their homeroom teacher in middle school. Ajax, a practical joker by nature, took the cleaning powder and with an eraser he pressed the powder all over the chalkboard. When the teacher had the classroom monitor clean the board later that day, the student found herself cleaning up a soapy mess.

In Tilt, Ajax and Gus really were not looking for girls, and since the establishment was almost empty, Ajax made another suggestion.

"Let's go to Likety Split," said Ajax.

"I don't want to see any naked ladies," Gus said.

"Oh, come on. You've never been," Ajax persisted.

"And I'm not interested. I love my wife," Gus said.

"What? You scared 'ole Mave'll find out?"

"No, I'm just not interested in goin'."

His friend flicked his ears, goading him on, "Come on. See somethin' new. Come on."

Before he could argue any more, Gus sat for a minute, picked up his cap, and followed his friend out of the establishment to the gentlemen's club. Likety Split was everything Gus imagined and more, with mirrors on the wall and comfortable, tacky, brightly colored red, purple, and royal blue décor. Scantily clad girls served drinks to customers, some young, but most were middle-aged and older men. Gus had never seen so many barely dressed, gorgeous women in one place in his life, but April caught his eye, not because she was particularly beautiful but because she reminded him of his wife.

Gus's father warned him about the dangers of tittie bars, but he did not understand until April started chatting him up. She was sexy sweet, and while she sipped on her drink, he watched her lips, fascinated by the glossy shade of bubble gum pink lipstick.

He asked, "Why are you in here dancin' naked?"

She smiled, "Son, this is not the place for that discussion." She then added, "I gotta go. I'm next."

When she got up to dance, he watched, staring into her eyes. At first she was looking toward the crowd. Her gaze met his. Something in the way she watched him drew him closer to the stage. His buddies were yelling in the background, cheering him on. Gus did not take out any money, so his friend pressed a one in his hands. April bent down, and Gus tucked the small bill in the nook of her breast, almost entranced with her pretty smell. He almost touched her breast but caught himself. Gus then moved away from the stage and let her dance.

"Come on," she whispered in his ears quietly after she finished dancing.

He looked at her, "What?"

April pulled him into a small, darkly lit room with a small chair. She gyrated in front of him and he just watched her, the sweat beading on his forehead. She came closer, and she turned so he now saw her backside moving in the same sensual motion. She began to glide her body against his, giving rise to his most sensitive part. His instinct was to reach for her breasts, but he ran his hand down the curves of her body, lightly touching her. He was so scared and anxious all at the same time that his nervousness began to show.

"Settle down. This is supposed to feel good," April purred. Mave then flashed before his eyes, and he pushed April away.

"Here," Gus handed the girl a twenty. "I can't do this. I…I'm married."

"Lots of married men do this, sweetheart. It's okay."

"I know, but I love my wife!" Gus said. Gus left the confused woman and left his friend in the joint. He walked home, the sweat pouring down his face. He passed Mave on his way to the shower.

"You all right?" she asked.

"Yeah, too much to drink."

Gus understood Mave more than even she knew, and that is why what he did next was the hardest thing he had ever done to Mave, for Mave. He let her have her freedom.

Chapter Thirty-nine—A Favor

At first Mave did not think she was doing anything wrong. An open spot on the board of directors at the local chamber of commerce was a rarity, as most remained in those seats until they retired or moved. When she appealed to Jolene to throw her vote Gus's way, she did so because she was aware that the only other qualified person would be Coreen's husband, Chuck. Actually, Chuck would have been a better fit, as his breadth of knowledge and business acumen were much more aligned with what the community would have benefitted from and would have needed. Gus was no slouch either, but to make sure, Mave thought it not only wise but normal business practice to appeal to those who could put in a good word for Gus.

"Mave, it's really not ethical. Actually I shouldn't be talkin' about it with you. I just want to let you know that Gus has just as good a chance as Chuck. You shouldn't worry," Jolene said.

Mave was over at the Hanson ranch for midafternoon tea, and she was trying to find a way to ask Jolene for the thing she needed without sounding immoral.

Mave said, "Oh okay. It's just—it's just."

"What, Mave? It's just what?" Jolene asked.

"Did you hear Coreen's boy, the one in college, is dating a colored gal?" Mave said, while waiting for the news to register with Jolene.

Mave asked this question knowing the only other serious competition for the spot on the board was Chuck. Mave knew Jolene, and she knew Jolene's racial sensibilities and sensitivities.

While Hickshaw had been almost fifteen years past the Civil Rights movement, it could have been one hundred years, as most people in town—both colored and white—kept an invisible but cordial boundary separating the races. Mave and Jolene were no different than the rest of the residents in Hickshaw. Both women came from families where intolerant, racial attitudes were not frowned upon, and so both women held onto their biases. For Jolene, the bias was against miscegenation.

"Oh yeah, she was complaining about her boy to us after church, worried about her bringing the gal to church," Jolene said. She continued, "But the gal is a high yella, looks almost white."

Sipping on her tea, Mave said, "Doesn't matter. One drop and she's still colored."

"I suppose yer right, and how would that look at the chamber Christmas party? All of us as white as snow with one black spot," Jolene said.

"I heard you can't tell with her. These times are changin'. I swear, sometimes you can't tell who you're dealin' with," Mave said.

Jolene turned to Mave and said, "All right, Mave. I'll see what I can do for you but no freebies."

"Okay, what do you want?"

"It's not that I want anything in particular. Well, I want you to tell me about Shirley," Jolene said. Fifteen years separated Mave and Shirley, and even with the occasional visit, the loyalty that was the glue holding Mave and Shirley had disintegrated.

"What do you want to know?"

"Why'd she leave?" Jolene asked.

"I never told you this story?"

"No."

"She was engaged to Duck, but right before they were t'get married, she decided she didn't want to be married. I don't think she ever wanted to be married in the first place," Mave said and then added, "Shirley's a different kind of woman, I suppose."

"What do you mean different?"

"When we were younger, most girls would try to get the boys to kiss them by playing tag. Shirley, I guess, was always running from them."

"You think she's lesbian?"

"Naw, I don't think it's that. I just don't think she was mature enough to be married."

"Didn't she use'ta have a thing for Jamie?"

"Funny you say that because Gus thought the same thing," Mave said and then she added, "Why do you ask?"

"I dunno. Did Duck even like her?"

"Look, Jolene, I don't know what transpired between the two of them. I think Duck liked her a lot. I know he was real disappointed. If you're askin' me if your husband misses a girl who he probably would not have even known much less married, I can't answer that. The story is there is no story," Mave said, and then she looked at Jolene and said, "I'm sorry. There isn't more."

"Well, it's all right."

The two sat facing the sun while discussing other politics of Hickshaw. Around 4:30 p.m., Mave climbed into her pickup and headed north in the direction of Macon.

Gus would be appointed to the board of directors at the Chamber of Commerce in Hickshaw despite Chuck's excellent qualifications, and Mave would never question her conversation with Jolene.

Chapter Forty—Marla Makes Good

In her thirty-second year, Marla took stock of her life. She had a thriving social life, but ultimately she desired a husband and a family. She had been seeing Davis for almost two years and he was a perfect fit. Even so, she was still recovering from her first attempt at matrimony.

When he said, "Honey, I want to marry you," she could hardly believe her ears. She shared everything about herself with him, except the one reason for her not being married.

"I need to tell you somethin'."

"What, is it that serious?" Davis asked.

"Well, it's somethin' I think you should know." Marla went on to tell him about her first marriage attempt.

"I'm glad you told me, but it doesn't change how I feel about you," Morrison said.

"I know. I just want you to know that about me."

"Do you realize that was almost fifteen years ago?" he asked.

"Yeah."

"Come here." He then reached out to touch his fiancée and said, "You're not that person anymore."

A long time had passed since she had someone remind her of that point. Marla had gone home rarely because Hickshaw was like a mirror constantly telling her in so little many ways she was not the fairest one of all. This time, with Davis's agreement, she married the way all the women in her town did—at church.

Her wedding was a simple affair, the colors reflecting a maturity and style of the bride with a soft pastel pink and a touch of eggshell dotted here and there. Her parents and sister loved Morrison, so getting the two families together was not difficult. The day began as a sunny, hot summer one. The ceremony and exchanging of rings went off without a hitch. Marla found it wonderful to see the people she grew up with, including Shirley, in attendance. Even though Shirley was her sister's close friend, Shirley understood Marla a lot more than Mave did.

"I just don't understand what she's thinkin' when she sleeps with these men," Mave explained to Shirley, exasperated about Marla's unwillingness or lack of desire to settle down. At the time, Marla had a series of boyfriends. Each time she broke up with the boy, the reasons ranged from the man boring her to him not spending enough money on her.

"Maybe she thinks she likes them," Shirley said about Marla.

"You can't expect a man to marry ya if yer given it to'm for free," Mave stated plainly. Mave reconsidered her words, "Hon, I'm sorry. You don't even wanna to marry."

"I never said that," Shirley said.

"Well, then what's the issue? We were always told why buy the cow if you can get the milk for free?" Mave said.

Shirley started laughing, "It's not about cows or milk."

"Then what is about?"

"Mave, some people are not meant to marry, to have children. Maybe it's not so important to her. It wasn't so important to me, either. That is why I left."

Shirley understood what it was like to just want to be with someone without worrying about whether the person was going to respect her enough to commit to her. To Marla, these hassle-free relationships seemed the most fun, with both parties knowing where the other stood. The world made the failure of relationships a heavy burden for a woman to carry. For this reason, Marla made her relationships simple and faultless, and Shirley understood Marla.

Because of her perspective on courting, Marla returning home to get married was extra sweet. She did not tremble at the thought of being thirty-two-year-old bride. She embraced it. All the years she put into dating all types of men, she felt confident about this man.

After the ceremony, she and a group of her bridesmaids headed out by the live oak and talked shop. Shirley, followed by a couple of the women from her high school graduating class, came over to the oak tree and sat. The weather had turned to a five o'clock, 100-degree swelter, so the slight breeze under the shaded tree was a welcome to the women—both married and single—while they watched the men put up the tents for the evening's festivities. All seemed to be having a good time, the conversation ranging from the new style in frosting hair to college hopes for the young ones.

Out of the corner of her eyes, Marla noticed Mave, Jolene, and similar types glowering in their direction. She turned her back, not taking a second glance. She was in love on her wedding day, and in hours, headed to Bali to consummate her marriage. Whatever was eating at Mave would be on hold until she returned. Life was good and not even her dearest sister would rain on that.

Chapter Forty-one—Love

Shirley sat under the oak with Mave and the other women, listening to the married women converse while feeling like a young girl and wondering if she would ever wear the veil. This thought took her to another time when she and Jamie sat under this same tree discussing their own futures.

"I'm gettin' married," Shirley said while looking at Jamie under her eyebrows.

This announcement shocked Jamie because in the time that they had been hanging out together after school, she had never mentioned a boyfriend much less getting engaged to a boy.

"Oh yeah, what's his name?" he said, expecting her to fabricate a boy, as he had known a girl to do that to get his attention.

"Duck."

Jamie laughed. He went to school with Duck, or Edward Chester Hollingsworth, he shot marbles with him in the schoolyard as eighth graders, and he even smoked in the bathroom with him after lunch. Even so, he was not impressed with him.

"Whose idea was that?" Jamie asked cynically.

"Whatdaya mean by that?"

"Oh, come on, Shirley. Everybody knows that Mave is getting married at the end of the semester. It just seems kind of—"

"Kind of what?"

"Sudden."

"Yeah, well, sudden or not I'm gettin' married too."

They both sat quietly for a few minutes while it registered with Jamie. Shirley could hardly believe it herself. The week before she was thinking about whose team she preferred to play on during gym, the boys or the girls, and as of the previous Sunday, she had a wedding to plan. Planning the whole wedding part did not bother her—that would be fun. Sex bothered her. She never had sex, and she did not find it too interesting. When she thought about Duck, she found it rather revolting. Shirley then turned to Jamie, who looked rather pensive.

"What are you thinkin' on?" she asked.

"I don't know. Do you even like him?" Jamie asked.

"I've known Duck since elementary school, and he's nice."

"Shirley, he's nice, but do you like him or even love him?"

"I don't know. I don't know if I ever have been in love with anyone."

Jamie was looking at her, very deeply disturbed by this time, and trying to figure out a way to stop her from making this mistake. He liked Shirley, but she was a different sort. He could not just hold her hand or even kiss her. Instead, he would do the things like wrestle her to the ground or chase her with frogs and other bugs, things that would place him in her space and in close proximity for him to touch her without scaring her off. He tried once to kiss her, and she kind of looked at him blankly.

"Jamie, what are you doin'?" she asked, knowing what he wanted but too afraid to let him do it.

"Nothin'," he said. He then let her go, but his heart still beat fast for her. In this moment, though, he wanted to tell her to not marry Duck. Duck knew nothing about her. Duck would not be able to really understand her, but instead providence opened the door for him.

"There is one thing that bothers me," Shirley said.

"What?"

"Sex," she looked at him, and she thought he was smirking.

"Stop laughing. Seriously, Jamie, I've never even kissed a boy, and I don't know if I even wanna have sex."

"Are you serious? Shirley, you have to have sex with your husband. It's like the law."

"I know, but I don't really wanna. I could handle the kissin'. It's just everything else."

"You never have been kissed?"

"No. I mean, you're the only boy I really hang out with," she said. Then she added, hoping he would not laugh at her, "The only thing I know about kissin' is people slobber all over each other."

"Shirley, it's more than that."

"That's all I've ever seen Mave and Gus do."

There was more silence between the two and then he turned to her. "I could teach you," he said quietly.

"What? Jamie, are you puttin' the moves on me?"

"No, you want to know how to kiss and I know how. I could show you. I've kissed lots of girls."

"I know," Shirley said. She did not say anything for a while because she wanted to kiss him, but she did not know if it would be all right.

"Okay," Shirley said and Jamie looked at her with incredulity.

"Shirley Carmicheal, are you actually going to let me teach you something?"

"I'm gonna need to know how, Jamie. Come on, be serious."

"What about Duck? He might not like me slobbering all over his wife."

"Oh, come on, Jamie. It's just a kiss."

"All right," he said. Jamie looked at her and opened his mouth to kiss her. His lips touched her open lips, which were tense.

"Relax your lips, silly."

"Okay," she said.

Jamie kissed her. The taste of Dr. Pepper was fresh in his mouth and his lips felt good to her, but being this close to Jamie felt weird to Shirley. She never had anyone's body pressed against her in this way. His arms were sinewy, and at first she felt awkward, but then she let go and began to kiss him back softly. Still kissing her, Jamie knew at some point she would stop him, and it would have tortured him to stop. After about five minutes, he attempted to kiss her on the neck, but she pushed him away.

"Jamie. Jamie."

"What?" He kept kissing her on the neck.

"Stop. I gotta stop. I'm supposed t'git married," Shirley said, touching his cheek. He pushed himself away.

"I'm sorry. I must've gotten carried away with myself," Jamie said.

"It's okay," she said. She looked down at the grass they were sitting on.

He then said, "I'm sorry. I shouldn't have done that."

"It's okay," she said quietly. "So what are your plans after school?"

"The military."

"You wanna be a soldier?"

"No, I want to travel, but the military is going to get me there."

"Gosh, that's seems kind of exciting."

"It will be. I can't wait to get out of here. I hate this town," he said.

"Oh Jamie, has it really been that bad here?"

"Yes, Shirley, you know what my life is like here with the craziness of my mother and all." This time was the first he ever mentioned his mother or anything related to the rumors.

"Oh, Jamie, those are just rumors, and no one really thinks about that crap anymore anyway."

"Some of them are rumors. Some of them aren't. Anyway, after graduation, I'm outta here."

"Will you miss me?" Shirley asked.

Jamie looked at her. She did not know why she asked that question, but she liked him and just needed to know that everything in Hickshaw had not all been terrible for him.

"Of course," he said and then paused. "You should come with me."

"What? Jamie, I'm gettin' married."

"Come on, Shirley. You don't even want to get married."

"I know, but I am."

"Think about it," he said, and then he added, "We better get going. You have a wedding to plan and, well, Marie Sue and me are supposed to get together later."

She knew Jamie was dating Marie Sue but that last comment stung her, and while she was supposed to get married, she liked Jamie a lot. With the taste of his wet kiss on her lips, she stood up and faced Jamie.

"I don't need to think anymore. I'm goin' with you."

She did not know how she would swing it, but right there in that moment, she knew that she wanted be with Jamie doing the same thing he would be doing, becoming the person he would and maybe becoming the one he ultimately wanted. That was almost eighteen years ago, and while Shirley sat under the oak tree, she wondered how far life had taken him from the thing he most wanted.

Chapter Forty-two—A Southern Live Oak

The next day after church, Shirley felt a chill from Mave she had never felt in the almost forty years she had known her. Normally, Mave would take her place by Shirley in church when she came to town, but Jolene, Duck, and their family had occupied that space. Shirley had not thought about the previous night's diversions, except that she was glad Marla was finally happily married. Shirley figured it was Mother's Day and the mothers in the church decided to sit together. She hardly had a chance to speak with Mave because Mave had been quite busy at the wedding, and during the reception most of Shirley's time was spent dancing and socializing, as Shirley had not been home in a while and some people could not get enough of her. When church was over, she had a chance to say a quick good-bye to Mave, head home to spend the rest of the day with her family, and then get back on the road to Tampa.

"Mave," Shirley said, lightly tapping Mave on the shoulder.

"Oh, hey," Mave said.

"I wanted to say good-bye, seeing as I have to head back to Tampa soon after we eat."

"Actually, I need to speak with you as well," Mave added in an authoritative tone. Shirley watched Mave move away from the gaggle of women that surrounded her, them each giving Mave a supportive glance.

"What's up?" Shirley asked, thinking Mave was going to ask her for some favor.

"I really don't know how to say this, with you being my oldest and dearest friend," Mave stumbled. "But I figured since you're from here you already know about it by now."

"Know about what?"

"The oak," Mave said and then pursed her lips. "The live oak that us married women sit under."

For as long as her family lived in Hickshaw, the rule that married women were the only one allowed under the shaded space of the hundred-year-old Southern live oak tree after a wedding was one that was rarely, if ever, broken. Even though its branches radiated far out enough to shade the whole town if necessary from the searing heat of the sun, married women held a special place under that tree, guarding the perimeter of the tree from children and other interlopers.

"You have to be kiddin' me, Mave. Everybody was under that tree." Shirley continued, "It was more than 100 degrees out there yesterday, and Marla didn't seem to mind it."

"Marla, going through all she has, watched another woman take her seat under that very same tree and didn't make any bones about the rule," Mave said.

Shirley returned, "Marla is a different type of woman."

"Still, it's for married women."

"So you expect us single ladies to bake in the hot sun because circumstance has it we aren't married? Well, let me ask you this, Mave Michaelson. What have you done in this world that is so great that gives you the right to deny me a space in the shade, other than gettin' married and havin' kids, that is?" Shirley asked, quite perturbed with

Mave's demand.

Mave's face turned fire engine red, and by now all the women were standing on the ground quietly listening to the argument. Shirley and Mave stood on the church porch, each standing their ground.

"Shirley, you had a chance to marry, but you didn't, so don't sit here and make us feel like we are punishin' all single women because of what you done!" Mave said, pointing her finger at Shirley.

"Maybe I wanted more'n this life, Mave. Maybe I didn't want to be Jolene!" Shirley said and then stopped talking, aware that the Jolene stood among the women watching the spectacle of their lifelong friendship being played out in front of Mave's friends. The women, sensing the seriousness of the argument, dispersed, each one going to her own vehicle. After one of the women told Mave that she would be heading along home, Mave finished saying good-bye hurriedly to Jolene, Coreen, and Josie. Shirley sat on one of the stairs of the church looking at a run making its way up her pantyhose. Mave came back to where Shirley sat, and Shirley stood up.

"Have you no sense? What? That education of yours has dimmed your common sense," Mave said and then continued. "Jolene, I'll have you know, has been a very good friend to me in your absence!"

Shirley sat quietly listening to her friend's anger.

"You coulda been educated too, but you didn't wanna miss out on that grand plan to marry," Shirley added. "Mave, it was not like you couldn't go to school. You chose this life, so don't get mad at me if it didn't work for you."

"It's not about being educated. You were just plain mean to her. Anyway, when you left, she was the only person I could talk to, so I'm not gonna set here and listen to you slander her."

"I have hardly slandered her, Mave. I just said I didn't want her life!" Shirley screamed.

Mave lowered her voice. "Anyway, regardless, I expect you to respect that we need space to talk. There are some things single women should not be privy to or wouldn't even understand," she continued. "What makes this so maddening is you had the opportunity to marry!"

"Not everyone is supposed to marry, Mave," Shirley said. "And let's not forget the conditions under which you got married were hardly conventional." The words flew out of Shirley's mouth before she could catch them.

"Conventional?" Mave asked.

"Traditional," Shirley explained.

Shirley did not mean to hurt her friend, but that sentiment had been hanging in the air since the first time Mave lectured Shirley on how to keep a man interested. The words stung, and it registered all over Mave's face.

Shirley continued, "I'm sorry. I didn't mean that. I'm sorry, Mave."

Mave asked, "Well, what the hell did you mean by it?"

The next couple words Shirley stated as plainly as possible because this sentiment is what she felt all these years. "You have chosen to live your life like everyone else in Hickshaw, making hell out of heaven for the rest of us."

Mave trembled with anger. "We still have to behave ourselves."

"All right. I'll remember to comport myself better next time." Shirley decided to let it go because this conversation was not one she was going to win.

"What do you mean comport?" Mave asked.

"Behave," Shirley stated flatly.

Shirley realized then what this conversation had really been about. She looked up to see Mave standing under the church awning while she stood on the bottom stair. A vision of a seventeen-year-old

Mave flashed before her eyes, black curls falling loosely around her face tired of being restrained by the rubber band she wore customarily. As Mave, the woman, stood before her, her once youthful face held a countenance of judgment. This picture softened Shirley's heart toward her friend so much so the only thing Shirley could do was walk up onto the awning where she and Mave stood. She brushed the obstinate curl behind Mave's ear and kissed her on her forehead.

Shirley said, "Maverick Michealson, I apologize for wrecking the tradition." Having not heard her given name since they were kids, Mave's voice cracked and it then softened as well. "It's just—" Mave trailed off.

"I know. I better go," Shirley said.

"I can give you a lift. I got the truck," Mave said.

"No, it'll be quicker for me to walk, seeing as I just live around the corner."

They said their good-byes, Shirley feeling a little more distanced from her friend and Mave, and glad she had restored order to her world. Shirley hopped over the porch railing on the side of the church and walked the same path she did almost eighteen years previously. She passed the massive oak tree with a trunk thick with age, letting the green shade cool her. Shirley went into the woods led by the path where she met Jamie that May night almost eighteen years ago. She looked back to see Mave already in her car heading in the direction out of town. Shirley went home to celebrate Mother's Day with her family and then went to Tampa.

On the ride home, Mave reconsidered her attitude about the oak. She did not mean to hurt Shirley, but for generations that was the town tradition. Shirley had run off and become this person who did not care about order or comporting herself properly around good folk, and what is worse, she expected everyone to be the same way.

While Shirley had become an educated woman, she never understood this tradition. In the past, when the town was settled almost 174 years ago, settlers came to the town with their brides. To avoid offending a husband, the married women were confined to the oak during town events so as not to confuse an unmarried woman from a married one. As the town progressed, the tree was a place where married women socialized, even though Shirley felt the rule was unfair and outdated.

Mave had to admit times had changed, but not to the point that traditions that had been a part of the town for decades should be discarded without respect for the past. With the tradition clearly reestablished, Mave still did not understand, even after Shirley's apology, why Mave remained so very angry with her friend. She did not understand how her feelings, which had been motherly toward her friend, had turned so sour so fast to the point of yelling at her about a tree, which they had played under as kids.

Tearing down the dirt road, the red clay kicking up dust behind her, Mave soon became consumed with a realm within her understanding, that being her home. As she drove into the driveway of the life she had built with Gus, she noticed an eerie silence that engulfed the property. Gus's truck was parked in the driveway and the garage door was open, but the kids were not there. Mave parked next to him and walked into a Mother's Day she had not planned for.

Chapter Forty-three—Departures

J amie counted the days until Francesca would leave. After seventeen years together, he was still fatherless, and he no longer was enamored by the childless couple lifestyle. He and Francesca could well afford to care for a child, but he, for some reason, was still fatherless. He never imagined his life leading him in this direction, but here he was sitting in the restaurant watching his wife wait tables and waiting for her to conceive. Tired of watching his wife serve meals to people, he walked out to the front patio of the restaurant where he saw another couple talking intimately. He sat at one of the tables, looked out on to the street, and reminisced about an earlier time.

Jamie walked in from school. Sullenly, he walked into a house in a mood about Shirley getting married. As he walked to his room, his mother and Johansson sat at the table eating dinner.

"Running late today," Johansson said.

"Yeah, I got held up with Shirley," Jamie said. He placed his jacket and books down on the countertops, and then he sat down at the table with his mother and her boyfriend. He helped himself to the contents of the various dishes on the table, and then he listened as the two adults conversed about the day's events.

"The Jackson boy got work over in Macon after high school,"

Johansson said.

"Oh, really? So soon after high school? Boy, his mother probably has connections in the city."

"No, I know Juliette, and she's been ridin' that boy since he was a freshman to get a job," Johansson said, and then he turned to Jamie. "What about you? Got any plans after high school?"

"Probably find something around here," Jamie said.

"Not gonna find too much in this area," Johansson said.

"Why not? There's plenty of work."

"Yeah, if you're into flippin' burgers over at Patsy's," his mother said.

"What do you mean by that?" Jamie asked.

"It's just this is a small community, and people aren't really into hirin' outsiders," Johansson said.

"We're not outsiders. Mom is from here, and I've lived here for seven years. We're hardly outsiders."

"Still. Havta have connections."

"Hey," Jamie's mother asked. "You know what you could do? What about the military?"

Jamie thought about the military but only fleetingly. He did not like Hickshaw, but he did not really want to leave his mother. Most boys his age and in his circumstance would see this as an opportunity to escape, and in the past couple of years, between the arguing and fighting about the different men in his mom's life, he yearned for the day he would finally be free to leave Hickshaw. Here was his opportunity to live a happy, good life like the ones that had been reflected back to him. Sitting with his mother and makeshift father, he was not so sure he wanted to leave home.

"Haven't really thought about it to tell you the truth," Jamie said.

"I think it's a great idea. I mean, ya get to travel the world, see new places, meet new women—" Johansson trailed off.

Jamie did not say anything, and the three sat at the table each having their own separate thoughts and ideas as to what Jamie would actually do. Mama was tired. She had been a mother for more than half her years, and she was not quite forty. She did not want her children living up under her, waiting for life to come along and take them somewhere. Her daughters were gone and had been married for some years, but Jamie seemed to want to just hang around. Maureen needed her space. She and Johansson were becoming an item to the point that they were actually going out together as a couple, something she had not experienced since she had been married to Jamie's father.

Johansson welcomed Jamie's impending graduation. He was tired of having to tiptoe around this boy about the arrangement Johansson had gotten used to while also knowing the boy went to school with his daughter. Johansson did not care about the talk in town, but the look of conviction in Jamie's eyes as he tried to guide the young man in his every day interactions screamed hypocrite! He just did not want to look in that mirror anymore, so after dinner that evening, he excused himself so that Jamie's mother could finally have the conversation with the boy that the two of them previously shared privately. The knock on Jamie's door interrupted a thought about Shirley.

"Knock, knock. Can I come in?" Maureen asked.

When Jamie did not answer, she walked in. The room was filled with a lingering hint of smoke, Jamie taking a drag of the last of his pot stash and putting the rest of the unsmoked bud in the ashtray underneath his bed.

"You haven't been smokin' pot in here, have you?" She asked. He still did not answer.

"Jamie, you know how I feel about that stuff. You could get arrested."

"What do you want, Mom?"

"Don't ignore my question, Jamie. I mean it. I want you to cut that shit out."

"Okay," Jamie said. Maureen looked around the room before searching for the words that would decide his future.

"Me and Billy think the military would be good for you."

"What? Mom! Are you serious?"

"Why not, Jamie? It'd be so good for you to get out from under Hickshaw."

"Mom, I don't want to go into the military. I'm not even the type. You know how I hate following directions. I would never last."

"Give it a chance. You'll get to travel, meet new—"

"I know. You and William said that at dinner. I'm not interested."

"Jamie, this is not an option."

"What?"

"Unless you have a better alternative," she said with her hand on her hip.

"Why can't I stay here?"

"I don't want you hangin' 'round here doin' nothin'. You need to contribute to your own financial welfare. Get out there and do somethin' with yer life."

"You let Denise and her boyfriend—" Jamie said in reference to his older sister's living arrangement with her boyfriend just before they moved out on their own.

"Fiancee," his mother interrupted.

"—stay for about a year, and she didn't have a job," Jamie said.

"She was gettin' married, and they were tryin' to save money. It's not the same," Maureen said.

"I don't want to go into the military."

"Well, you can't stay here."

"What? Whose idea was this? Billy's?"

"It doesn't matter."

"He's making you do this."

"It wasn't just his idea," she said and then sat down on his bed. She ran her hand through his hair like she did when he was little.

"It's time for you to grow up, Jamie. I can't support us both forever," she said. He did not say anything. Then he moved his head from under her touch.

"It's Mama's turn to live her life," Maureen said softly. Jamie stood up and looked at her.

"I don't want to go," Jamie said. She got up quickly and went to the door.

With one hand on her hip and the other on the door handle, she said, "You have to find some way to support yourself Jamie. You can't stay here."

He picked up his jacket and looked at her.

"Fine," Jamie said and flew past her and out the door where he bumped into Johansson on the way to the car.

"She's all yours," he said.

Johansson stood there, not knowing quite what to make of the few words that Jamie spoke to him. A few weeks after this encounter, Jamie and Shirley were driving to Macon. Jamie knew had he remained in Hickshaw he would have been a father by now.

Chapter Forty-four—Henriksen Flooring and Decks

This Mother's Day, Mave hurried home from church to make a feast for her family. Usually the kids sat in the living room and watched her cook after she opened her Mother's Day gifts, but this day, Mave stepped into the cool air-conditioned home. She was headed toward the refrigerator for a cool drink when taped to the handle of the door was a small card. She opened the card, a traditional card much like the ones given on days like this one. The note inside read:

My Dearest Mave,

This Mother's Day I'm giving you the gift of freedom. I don't know what else to give you that will make you happy. For a long time, there has been a hole in our marriage—

Mave pulled out one of the chairs in the den and processed Gus's letter. As she let the separation sink in, Gus walked through the washroom. She looked up at him, waving the card before him.

"Honey, yer not gonna to leave me, are you?"

"Mave, it's not gonna to work. You know more'n I, this is not a marriage." Gus pulled up a chair close to his wife and said, "I've loved you, Mave, longer and deeper than I've felt in this life."

"But then why?"

"It's like livin' with a child, you hangin' half out of the marriage," he continued. "Then there's thing about Atlanta and you goin' to school. I'm just tired. I can't keep up anymore."

Mave asked, "Atlanta?"

"Yes, Mave, I know about Bruce," Gus said softly.

Mave turned crimson reflecting back on the slow dance almost four years previously.

"It's not what you're thinkin', and about school, I put that away a long time ago."

"There are pamphlets for University of Georgia, Mave."

"That's for Chet."

"This literature is not for Chet. He does not want to go to college," Gus explained softly.

"How do you know?"

"I know my children," he said, watching the tears roll down his wife's face. "Mave, there are some things you need to do on your own to make you happy. Me and my children are just standin' in the way. You don't need me."

"They are my children too, and yes, yes, I do need you. Please don't leave me," she begged.

Gus, now facing his wife, picked up her chin and said, "I love you, but I can't be with you, not like this. I want you to do what makes you happy for once."

He then kissed her, but in a husbandly way, their lips interlocked in longing he had not felt in a while. He left then. Mave sat for what may have been three hours mulling over in her mind whether Gus had been cheating on her and other possible reasons for his leaving. She got up to put some clothes together. She headed to Mama's. She could not stay in that lonely house. Putting clothes in an overnight bag, she glanced into the mirror at herself. She finally came into recognition that she had changed, her face taking on a look of permanent displeasure. Her eyes, once bright with life, were now dulled by years of disappointment. The eyebrows knitted in disapproval and created a fixed expression of judgment. Her perky lips finished the picture, as they now formed a pout. She had to wonder whether she always appeared this way to others.

Under this façade, she saw the eighteen-year-old girl. The made up face could not hide the vitality of the girl hidden by so many years of sacrifice and self-denial. When she got to Mama's, her mother, tired of worrying about her eldest daughter and long since putting to rest Mave's commitment to her marriage, said, "You can't stay here."

"What? Mama!"

"You can stay for the night, but your problems are not here. They are at home," her mother said. She added, "Mave, we've done you a great disservice by shaping your life for you," and kissed her on the forehead.

Her mother continued, "I don't think commiseratin' about Gus with us is gonna to help you. Yer a grown woman with three children and you need to figure this one out for yerself. Gus is givin' you the space to do it. You need to decide what's right for you this time—not me, not your daddy, or anyone else."

The next morning Mave awoke and headed home to put the pieces of her life together. As she walked into the home she and Gus decorated, she noticed the amalgam of school art on the fridge and the school and family portraits that aligned the walls of the home. She was sitting on Gus's side of the bed when the shine of his wedding band caught her attention. Then she opened the small hope chest, but not before noticing the college award certificate rolled up and Shirley's topaz ring. She placed Gus's ring in the box, another token of her life.

Mave then wept.

The next day, Mave woke up resolved to solve this marriage issue. She baked Gus a cherry pie—his favorite—and got herself all gussied up. She drove out to the Henriksen farm and waited until she saw his truck roll into the driveway. A couple of hours had passed and the pie was getting cold. She got out of the car and stepped onto the wide porch of the Henriksen household. A brief reflection of the times she and Gus spent on that porch as kids ran through her mind. The older Mrs. Henriksen, hearing a shuffling outside, opened the window to see her daughter-in-law standing in the dusty afternoon.

"Hello, Mave," her mother-in-law said, opening the door.

"Hi," Mave began nervously.

"Come on in."

"No, I just wanted to drop this off for Gus and the kids," Mave said and handed the pie to his mother.

"Are ya sure ya don't want to wait? Gus and the kids should be back soon."

"No, ma'am. I'm just here to drop this off."

She gave the confection to her mother-in-law and quickly descended the stairs. On her way out of the long driveway, she remembered the stream on the property the two of them used to swim in as kids and headed in that direction. There they were, Gus wrestling a now-grown Chet and the two girls on the sidelines, one cheering for Daddy and the other for Chet. The scene made her reconsider her actions of the last twenty years. She wondered whether she had so neglected her family to the point that they functioned perfectly fine without her. All of the bake sales, baseball games, and cheerleading practices did not seem to amount to much because here, right in front of her, Gus and her children formed a unit. At this point, she would need to do more than bake a cherry pie to get not only her husband back but also her entire family. She stayed for a minute longer when Charlene said to her father, "There's Mama!" Mave, not ready to deal with their questions, waved to Gus, started the car, and moved on home.

In the comfort and solitude of her home, Mave sat quietly. She focused her eyes on photo albums of her family she had put together over the years. Throwing together a peanut butter and jelly sandwich, she sat at the kitchen table, pouring over decades of old pictures of Gus and her as teenagers. One picture was of Gus holding her in his arms as if he were carrying her over some imagined threshold, she in a one-piece bathing suit and he in a pair of cutoffs. She studied the picture, reflecting on the summer before they married. They spent their entire summer vacation at that pond.

Mave moved onto the homecoming pictures. She wore a dress made of lace and satin. Everyone likened her to one of the old great Southern belles. She looked magnificent standing next to Gus, Shirley, and Jamie. Mave was blessed with fine features that made her face flawless. In fact, a person could hardly tell she put on anything but a touch of lipstick most days. After reflecting on homecoming, she turned to the final set of photos in that album, and these photos revealed for the first time the fear she had about her marriage. In the picture, she stood next to Gus, wide-eyed and six months pregnant in her mother's ill-fitting wedding gown. Gus stood next to her as worried as she was, but at least he appeared to smile, his hand placed around her expanding waist in the photo. Shirley was nowhere in sight.

Mave closed the album and reached for the second album. The first picture was of a sweat-drenched Mave holding the tiny ball that was Chet in a receiving blanket with Gus hovering over the two of them. Then there were more pictures, one of Gus and Chet and another of the family and Chet. She continued her review of the family albums in search of an answer. Pictures of the girls in their Pop Warner cheerleading uniforms brought a smile to her face. She remembered how happy it made Charlene to be a mascot in her own miniature copy of the same uniform Lux wore.

Mave did notice, though, while the first album had been filled with pictures of her, in the last two albums she had vanished from her own life. Pictures of Gus and the kids fishing, camping, and going to amusement parks filled the albums. While her image did show up every now and then, the only way she appeared to be a part of this family was through the genetic imprint on the faces of her children. Gus, she figured, probably did know his children a whole sight better than she did. Her mother was right. Getting her family back was her responsibility, and if she failed, this time the blame would lie on her shoulders.

Chapter Forty-five—A Picnic

Jamie, his two sisters and his father sat under the shade of the immense oak tree. They found a comfortable, dry spot on the ground. His father spread the blanket on the ground, and the four enjoyed the early spring weather. The girls got up and walked back to the car to get the picnic basket, and Jamie and his father sat on the ground, his father's back leaning against a tree.

"When you move back in, maybe we'll have time to go up north. You know, to do some fishing," Jamie said. His father sat quietly, upset that he could not reveal the truth of what transpired between him and Jamie's mother.

Instead his father said, "We'll see."

"You always say that, but we never do anything," Jamie said.

Not getting the response that he wanted, Jamie persisted. "Are you getting married again to someone else?"

"Why do you ask?"

"I dunno. Every time I say anything about you and mom getting back together you don't really say anything."

Before his father could even answer, his sisters came back with the food. That day, the four of them ate sandwiches and coleslaw the girls made and talked about the lives they wanted. Then the girls went out toward the forest to collect berries for a pie. Jamie had just turned eighteen, and this meal would be one of the last he had with his father before he left Hickshaw.

"Your mother and I are different people, very different."

"What do you mean?"

"It doesn't matter. It just didn't work out between us."

"Yes, it does."

"Jamie, your mother and I are no longer together and haven't been for over four years," his father said. The boy's face became sullen. His father wanted the boy to at least enjoy this day. Jamie would be leaving for the military in a couple of weeks, and the father did not know when he would see his son again.

"Look, Jamie, there are just some things you won't understand until you are older."

"Like what?" Jamie asked.

"Son, I don't want to spend our time together like this."

"Neither do I, but I don't want to leave Hickshaw without knowing."

"Knowing what, Jamie? What is it that you want to know?"

"Why you left, damn it!"

"Jamie, I don't think this is the place or the time."

"Why? Why? What did you do that was so bad that she threw you out! What?"

"I didn't leave, Jamie. Your mother wanted out!" his father said, and then he continued. "Damn it, Jamie. I didn't want you to find out like this."

This revelation upset Jamie, and for a moment, he said nothing.

"Your mother was not ready to commit to a life with me when we got married in the first place, and no, I'm not angry about it. It was probably for the best for all of us," his father said.

"It wasn't good and definitely wasn't for the best, at least not for me," Jamie said.

The rest of the afternoon after this revelation Jamie remained silent as his sisters talked with their father about their lives. After the visit, his father dropped the girls off at their respective lives, and then he dropped Jamie off at home. Jamie walked into the house to see Johansson and his mother on the couch watching television. He gave her a perfunctory glance and she asked, "How was lunch with Dad?"

Jamie walked past his mother and her boyfriend not answering her. He closed the door to his room and closed her off. For three weeks, he thought about what his father said to him regarding his mother. The night before he left for Macon, he expressed his disproval of his mother's choice to leave his father. He walked out to the living area where his mother sat watching Johnny Carson.

"Is Johansson with his family?" he asked.

"What do you mean by that?" his mother asked in an irritated voice.

Jamie did not answer, but instead he turned toward his mother. "Why did you leave Dad?"

The question stung and stunned her. Jamie's parents agreed that while they no longer shared a commitment, what transpired between them would never be discussed with the children, and up until now, that had been the case.

"What did your father tell you?" she asked, placing the palm of her hand on her forehead.

"The truth."

"Jamie, that was so long ago. I'm not gonna to bring up ancient history."

"Then don't lie, Mom. I'm tired of hearing you talk about him like he was wrong for leaving, when come to find out, you left."

"What?" she screamed. She had already been pissed about Johansson not spending time with her. Johansson was still in the family way, and he chose to spend this particular Friday night with his wife and daughter. "Your father screwed around too, if you must know!"

Jamie looked at her in exasperation.

"Why are you like that?" he yelled back.

Jamie did not give her the chance to answer the question. He went to his bedroom where he began to pack his belongings for the trip north. The next afternoon he packed his belongings into the truck his father helped him build and walked past Johansson and his mother, not saying a word to either of them. Later that evening, he waited for Shirley by the side of the road behind the church on the path they took home from school.

Jamie thought about this time in his life, as Francesca tried to explain why things would not work between the two of them. They had been together nineteen years when he came home to find supper cooked and Francesca in the bedroom packing her things instead of on the love seat, as usual.

"I don't want this kind of marriage, Jamie."

"What? What am I doing?"

"Do you know what it really means to marry someone?"

"Yes, what is it that you want?"

"Jamie, you don't trust me."

"I do trust you. Francesca, I don't understand why you would just leave."

"You wouldn't even tell me about your family situation until we went to your home."

"I didn't think you would understand and that was almost twenty years ago."

"And there are other things."

"Like?"

"Your mother."

"Okay, what has my mother done now?"

"Jamie, you've heard her yelling at me. I don't know. I don't know. In my family, all my sisters get along with their mother in-laws. It's not perfect, but your mother—"

"My mother, what?"

"She doesn't, she isn't—"

"What? Francesca, what?"

"I can't even tell you this. Jamie, your mother has no respect for me as your wife."

"Don't say that."

"It's true, and it has affected our marriage. You don't tell me stuff so I won't get mad, and then I have to hear from her whatever secret you have kept from me. I'm not happy like this," Francesca said. "And then there is the thing about children."

"We—I—we agreed not to have children," Jamie said.

"Yeah, but, Jamie, you're not happy, and neither am I."

Jamie looked at her and the most profound sadness came over him, so he let her go. When he talked to his mother later that month, she consoled him. He never told her exactly why Francesca left, but his mother understood that, in some part, it was about her.

"I always had responsibility. I always took care of the younger ones, so when your father asked me to marry, I thought I was ready," his mother explained, and this time Jamie listened.

Maureen continued, "It was normal for us, at sixteen, to get married. Shoot, some thought you were lucky to be married so young."

"But?"

"But just after you were born, I began to see someone else," She explained, and Jamie was not so angry this time.

She said, "I didn't love the man I had the affair with, but I realized I couldn't stay married to your father. It wasn't fair."

"What about us?"

"I know, Jamie. It's better that I left, honey."

He would not understand his mother until much later, but this was the moment that Jamie forgave her.

Chapter Forty-six—Two Sides

I t's a gamble."

"I wish I knew that goin' in."

"Yeah, many folks don't realize what marriage is until they're into the thick of it," Mrs. Henriksen said, the warm breeze gently lapped over mother and son as they sat in rocking chairs on the porch, both of them gazing over into the acre of land where Gus's children played. Chet directed the girls on how to swing from the tire hung around the maple tree in the yard, and the girls half-listened.

"I just wish it hadn't come to this," his mother said.

"Mama, I didn't want to leave. I'm just tired. Plus, I figure since I'm the one who spends most of the time with the kids, what's keepin' her there?"

"I know, I know, I know. I just wished you'd talked to someone, Daddy or me, before you left."

"The house is kind of crowded. As soon as I can find some place and I figure out what exactly I want to do, we'll move," Gus said.

"It's not that, son. You're always welcome home. It's just we could have helped you sort through this before you left if you let us. Maybe it would not have come to leaving and divorcin' your wife."

"We're not gettin' a divorce. It's a separation. I think she needs space. That's why I just didn't get an apartment. Then Mave and me get back together and then I'm payin' on two homes."

"So, yer not really sure what yer gonna to do?" his mom asked with relief in her voice.

"I don't wanna to leave my wife, but there are some things she needs to work through. Some things neither you, Daddy, nor I can help her with."

"Well, what exactly is wrong?" his mother asked. Not one to interfere in the lives of her children, his mother was concerned that her baby, even though he was a man, was struggling with his marriage.

All Gus could say was, "Do you know how ugly it feels being with someone who is constantly trying to escape you?"

His mother pondered the question. She had no idea life and marriage had been this awful for Gus.

"What do you mean escape?"

"Mave doesn't want to be there, and I don't think she has from the beginning," Gus explained.

Not wanting to expose Mave's flaws, he did not assail her character with his mother by mentioning the times he thought she had been unfaithful to him or neglectful of the children's needs. His mother walked over to him and embraced him, kissing him on the cheek.

"I'm sorry for you. Marriage is good. I'm sorry you didn't get to experience that," she said and continued, "I gotta go make supper. You and the kids want anything special?"

"No, what you fix for Daddy is fine," Gus said. He stayed on the porch and considered his present position. Even though it had been the college brochures coming in the mail that had set him off, this separation had been a long time coming.

Often he would watch his wife with their children and become indignant by her haphazard care of them while never saying a word. She had this way where she seemed to perform the functions of a wife and mother as if it were another chore to complete in the day. He never saw her become too affectionate, but she provided his children with the basic care needed by a child from their parent. This custodial treatment of his family made him realize he deserved more and his children needed more. His youngest, a preteen, would be on her way to whatever life she planned for herself soon. Gus figured if they did divorce, then at least the kids knew what it was to belong to a two-parent family in their young lives.

Despite the feelings that festered in Gus, he still was protective of his wife, even at this strained time in the marriage. This protectiveness was apparent when Mave returned to church.

Having skipped the Sunday after their split, she came dressed in her usual wear. She walked into the church and was met by her mother and the newly married Marla. She stopped to chat with a few of her friends but the awkwardness was very apparent. Instead of the sympathy expected for a wife whose husband left her, she was the object of suspicion. Jolene and the girls knew Gus was not the straying type. Ultimately, it was something Mave had done because men do not leave without a reason. She sat in a pew next to Marla and her husband when Gus and the kids walked into the church. He saw Mave and already knew she had been shunned. With a million eyes watching them both, Gus did something that reflected goodness in his nature. He walked over to the pew where Mave sat listless, distraught at the possibility of her not being a married woman.

"Mave, honey, come sit with us."

"Gus, I can't. I don't want these people talkin' more than necessary. Let's just leave well enough alone."

"We're not divorced," he said quietly. "Now come join your family, at least for the kids' sake."

Gus slid into the pew next to her and then beckoned his children to come sit with the both of them. Gus was adamant, even in this moment when things fell apart, to at least present a united front. After church, Mave walked them to the truck.

"Gus, I need to have a moment with you."

"Okay. Chet drive your sisters to Patsy's and get some lunch," Gus said and handed the boy the keys and some cash to feed his younger siblings. Gus walked toward the shade of the live oak where they both felt the eyes of the community follow them.

"We need to figure out a time to talk about what we're gonna t'do," Mave said.

"I know," he said. "Can you meet this week?"

"Saturday morning will probably be better," she said.

"Okay," he continued. "Mave, we'll work through this, whatever it comes to."

Mave dropped Gus off at Patsy's, where she could see the waitress placing the heapings of burgers and fries before her children.

Chapter Forty-seven: Tête à Tête

Gus's voice rained down on Mave's, as she sat in the pew lost in her thoughts about the fragility of her position in the community. That she belonged to almost every committee in the church and had become a participating member of the chamber did not matter to her friends. Her relationships in the community fractured the minute these women found out her marriage was in turmoil.

"Are we gonna meet at Patsy's after chamber?" Mave asked Jolene after church, still trying to hold the vestiges of her life together.

"Well, yeah, but it's couples this time," Jolene informed her and moved onto another conversation with Josie, but not before saying, "I'll catch up with you later in the week."

Jolene did not have to say anything nor did she catch up with her later. Mave already knew the unspoken couple's rule, and they knew about her designation from wife to potential divorcee. Mave did not expect better because she had not heard from any of them in the previous weeks. She almost laughed at Jolene's response, seeing as the only reason Jolene got Duck was because the woman he should have married ran off. The other women were also source of Mave's derision. She remembered when Josie was on the verge of a breakdown because she was twenty-one and still not married.

This life was not the one Mave envisioned for herself. She made herself fit into this life. If not for the pregnancy, she would have been an educated woman. She never stopped seeing herself as that independent woman, even when it appeared that Gus kept saving her from this life, but the time for school had long passed. She really wanted her husband and family back more than she wanted the education. When she and Gus met the following Saturday, she would make that clear.

Saturday morning she got herself together, putting on a very low-cut, slinky summer dress. She went to Marla's the day before and fine-tuned the arches on her eyebrows, cut her black hair into fashionable ringlets, and had a pedicure and a manicure. Gus, already sitting at the booth closer to the back of the diner, saw the vision Mave transformed herself into. In previous days, Gus might have chucked the whole breakfast thing and gotten Mave home for some serious lovemaking. The desire did not stir in him this time, though, because he could not get the image of Mave as a teenager out of his mind.

When she sat down, he stated in a stern voice, "Mave, this is not gonna be that kinda meetin.'"

There was a minute of awkward silence, and then Mave said, "I don't wanna divorce."

"Well, then what is it that you want?"

"I wanna stay married!" she said. Gus looked out the restaurant window, frustrated.

"We're not kids anymore, Mave. It's more complicated than just not wantin' a divorce. Do you realize in a couple of years the littlest will be gone? Then what are we gonna do?" Gus asked.

Mave sat quietly, staring at the red acrylics she had applied the day before.

"I know, Gus." She added, "I suppose we do what other people have done, live."

"No, livin' is not good enough. That's what we've been doin' now and I, for one, am not happy."

Mave said to him, "I've done everything you've asked of me. I don't understand this."

Gus interrupted. "In many ways, you haven't been there. You cook and clean and make sure to take the kids to their appointments, but did you know Charlene is joining band and not cheerleading? Or that Lux has already made plans to attend a cookin' school in South Florida? Already been admitted but talkin' to you all of your children would be set for college." Each piece of information about her children was a hidden accusation.

"Do you wanna to know how I feel?" Mave asked.

"That's what I've been waitin' for."

"I was on my way to my own schoolin' years ago when I listened to you when you said you'd be with me forever."

"But not like this, Mave," he interjected.

"Let me finish," Mave said coolly.

"You led me to believe this," she said, raising her hands out in front of her, "was the life you wanted for us." Her voice was starting to rise.

"Lower your voice."

"And I gave it to you," she said quieter this time, pointing her finger on the diner's table.

"I didn't ask you to marry me because I wanted a housekeeper or a baby sitter. I wanted a partner in life."

In probably one of the most honest discussions they had together, Mave said, quite flatly, "I was pregn'nt, Gus. That's why you married me!"

"I know, but that's not why I married you. I loved you. I would've married you anyway!" he exclaimed. Mave looked over her shoulder to see if anyone heard. Only two of the waitresses were behind the counter watching the discussion.

Aggravated, she looked over her shoulder and shouted, "Don't you have some work to do? Stop minding my conversation." Then she turned to Gus and asked in frustration, "What is it you want from me then, Gus? I've given you everything," Mave said, almost crying. "Everything!"

"I want you to be the person you'd have been if I never stepped foot in your life," he added. "Because that's what I think will make you happy." He then slid out of the booth, said something to the waitress, and left.

Chapter Forty-eight—On Her Own Terms

Mave ate the breakfast of blueberry pancakes and sausage that the waitress brought to the table. The server gave her extras. Having been a server for years, the woman had seen her fair share of women trying to hold onto a man halfway out of the door. When Mave got up to pay the bill, she discovered Gus had already settled with the waitress on his way out.

Mave left Patsy's confused. She did not understand what it was Gus wanted. She put school away because that is what everyone told her would make her and Gus happy. She still wanted to go to school, but she so dearly wanted her family back. She did not understand what Gus feared about their entire marriage until one afternoon.

At Gus's job, Mave dropped off a form that needed a signature required for an insurance health policy application for the kids. As she approached the family business, Mave saw Gus's truck in the drive way, in addition his father's and their secretary's vehicles. At about half past one, Gus would take a break for lunch. She pulled out the hero sandwiches, chips, and iced tea she purchased at a local deli and headed inside the establishment to join him. She glanced quickly at the sign "Henriksen Flooring and Decks" and then entered the building. When she entered the office, Gus's secretary was sitting at the typewriter on her desk. She pointed Mave in the direction of the back where Gus was eating lunch.

Mave went out the front door and walked toward the back of the building. What she saw helped her understand why Gus had been who he was to her and why he left. Her stomach roiled with anxiety at what was before her. She did not know whether to leave or confront him. Just the sight of Gus sharing a meal with a woman who could not have been a day over twenty-five years old put her in the throes of serious worry and contemplation. Mave stood there for about five minutes to ascertain the nature of the relationship. She watched as Gus took sips of the soft drink and chatted with the young girl, occasionally throwing his head back in great laughter that exposed the Adam's apple Mave had kissed in their more intimate moments.

"What on earth could this girl be sayin' that is so damn funny?" she thought to herself. The food in her hand let off an aroma, reminding her that she probably needed to eat it or refrigerate it, so she dropped the forms off at the front desk and got back in her vehicle and went home. The sensation Mave felt was a tingly, not-so-good feeling she got when she was worried, scared, confused, and distracted all at the same time. Through all of these feelings, she could only concentrate on Atlanta and how Gus might have discovered Bruce. The only person who knew about Atlanta was Marla.

At this point, she paced the kitchen, taking bites off the sandwich she purchased. Then she picked up the phone.

"Why did you tell Gus?" Mave barked into the phone.

"What?"

"Why'd you tell Gus about that guy in Atlanta?"

"Mave, what in the heck are you talkin' about?" Marla asked.

"From the hair show," Mave said. Marla was silent on the other end of the line, trying to figure out just who and what Mave was talking about. Then it clicked.

"Oh, honey, I didn't tell Gus anything about that." Marla added, "Is that why he left?"

"He thinks I cheated," Mave said. "Are you sure you didn't say anything maybe by accident? I'm not gonna be angry. I need to know so I can figure out just what he knows and head this thing off."

Marla remembered her sister used to say "head this thing off" phrase to her when she would tattle on Mave and then be afraid to tell her older sister she was the source of the trouble. As the younger one, Marla looked up to Mave no matter what her sister did. She doted on her because Mave had been good to her as a sister. For this reason, it was difficult for Marla to be honest with her.

"Mave, has it ever occurred that he left because you keep secrets? I mean, look at what you just said. 'I need to know what he knows.'"

"Marla, you are in no position to judge."

"No, you're right. I've probably done the same thing, but I don't hide things from my husband," she said softly.

"Neither do I," Mave said and then thought back on the lunches at the school with Watson, the volunteering, and all the many different lies, omissions, and secrets she kept hidden from Gus over the years. Her voice softened as well.

"I'm sorry. I want to fix this and don't know how. I'm sorry. I shouldn't have called," Mave said and hung up the phone. She needed to talk to someone who truly understood.

Chapter Forty-nine—Maverick

S hirley."

"Hello, Mave."

"Gus left."

This call had been the first Mave made to her closest friend throughout life since her conversation with Shirley about the oak tree. Mave announced Gus's departure very quickly and bluntly, as though she were delivering news that she was not sure was good or bad. Mave knew Shirley liked Gus, but somewhere in the back of Mave's mind, she felt Shirley did not think Mave should have married in the first place. Mave did not sound worried, but her voice was tense.

"What?" Shirley asked.

"He left me. He took the kids. I don't know what to do. I'm really scared he's gonna divorce me."

"Mave, settle down. What happened? Start from the beginning," Shirley said. Shirley had just come from the beach, but her laid-back tone made Mave wonder whether she had company.

"Is there a man in there? Are you busy?" Mave asked.

"No, Mave. I've just come in from the beach. What's going on?"

"It's a long story but the jist of it is, he wants me to figure out what I need."

"Well, that's about twenty years too late," Shirley said. "I don't know what to say. I thought you two settled all of that years ago."

"I know. But it's more'n that," Mave said. "He thinks I cheated on him."

"Did you?"

"No, not really. It's a misunderstanding. I danced with this guy, and I don't know somehow Gus found out," Mave explained. "But that's not what I'm callin' about. I don't know what to do. I need help."

"Mave, I don't know. I've never married." Shirley paused to consider Mave's option and then said, "He said he wanted you to figure out what makes you happy."

"Yeah."

"It sounds like he's settin' you free."

"In the beginnin' I thought he was in the way. I don't think he meant to wreck my future, but I've always felt like he wanted to hold me back from somethin', somethin' that would be really good for me. Nonetheless, I love him and I don't wanna be free anymore," Mave cried. "And I have missed them so much since they've been gone."

"Them?"

"He took the kids, Shirley. This is serious," Mave said.

Shirley sat for a while, reassuring her friend that everything would work out fine.

Then she asked, "Why'd you marry?"

The question was a simple one that Mave never seriously considered in all the years she had been with Gus.

Shirley continued, "You didn't have to."

"I don't know, Shirley. Because Gus got me pregnant."

"Jeez, Mave, you act like he did it on purpose."

"I don't know, Shirley. After all these years, when I think about it, he might just have," Mave said.

Shirley sat on the other end of the phone, not sure how to feel or what to say.

"What makes you say this, Mave? I mean, that's serious."

"He's been so afraid of me goin' to school for one, and he wouldn't even let me work and develop a life outside of his. Part of me doesn't want to believe he'd do this to me but—I don't know what to think."

Ignoring Mave's comment, Shirley said, "Mary Jolsten got pregnant and didn't marry. She's doin' fine. So did Loren Johnson, who now owns a business." She continued, "You were running from shame, Mave. Being alone with a child without a husband was a little too scary for you. Wasn't it?"

"Shirley! That has to be the meanest you've ever said to me."

"I'm not trying to be mean," Shirley said. Still annoyed by Mave's edict about the live oak, she tempered her next comments. "It's like you've given all the power in your life over to Gus, like he stole the life you wanted from you and now that he's set you free, you're still not happy."

They both sat quietly, each on the other end of the line considering Shirley's comment.

Shirley said, "You want your husband back? Figure out why you married'm and why you stayed in the first place. It'll answer a lot of your questions about what you should do."

Mave did not understand the sourness in her friend's voice. While Mave saw this trial separation as a disadvantage, Shirley saw it as an opportunity.

"Don't you want me to be happy?" Mave asked.

"Yes. I'm sorry, Mave. I just don't see it as such a negative as you do. I think if you think about it, Gus has done you a favor." Understanding Mave may have not been ready to hear these words, Shirley continued, "Just talk. Tell me everything."

Mave did. Mave told her how she held onto that scholarship award certificate for years, sometimes glancing at it in darker moments of the marriage, and she talked about how suffocating their early marriage had been for her but how she loved Gus all through it all. Mave believed in the marriage. She talked about the attraction to other men, including Watson. Most importantly, she discussed in depth how she stifled any desire for learning to please not only Gus but also her family. Shirley listened and reflected on the sadness in Mave's letters.

Shirley sat on the other end quietly and then said, "Mave, a long time ago, you were on your way to the life you had been talkin' about since we were kids, and then it's like in one year all that changed."

"More like fifteen minutes," Mave said. The two chuckled.

"Okay. Fifteen minutes. Honestly speakin', I don't think you should've married'm at all but you did, and now you have built a life for yourself with Gus and you seem happy."

"No, I haven't been happy."

"Content, then. Let me finish. I think this is where you are at now, and the past is the past. You can't do anything to undo it, but you can only live now."

"Everybody regrets somethin'," Mave said.

"You're right. We all have regrets, but—I don't know. It seems like you're still eighteen waitin' to be freed from a permanent situation you thought was temporary. You've gotten so used to livin' temporarily that you never ever thought that Gus might let you go or might wanna be free from the same thing himself. I don't know. It just seems like if you want'm back, go get'm. But if he comes back, he's yours. You would have chosen this life for yourself this time—not him or your parents."

Mave digested this last piece of advice, swallowing hard on the bitter years of self-sacrifice and denial, the years of pretending everything fine when it was not. When Mave hung up with Shirley, the first thing she did was visit the small treasure box where she kept her personal items. The first item she removed was the awards certificate. Almost twenty years old, this relic was yellow with age and constant handling.

She went over to the fireplace and placed the certificate over the fire. While she fished out the other nonessential baggage of that previous existence, the certificate burned to cinders. The only items she kept from that time in her life was Shirley's topaz ring and Gus's wedding band. She did not need any more thought about what to do. She did not know who she would have been if Gus never stepped foot in her life. She was the person she had grown into because of Gus, and for Mave, that is all she could be.

After coming to a resolution, Mave decided to spend the better part of Sunday preparing a meal, even skipping church. When the chicken and dumplings, corn muffins, green bean casserole made with fresh green beans, and lemon almond pound cake had been prepared, she headed to the Henriksens' house, where she found her three babies, now almost grown, sitting on the porch.

"Charlene, Lux, Chet, come on. Get in the car. We're goin' home," she said. They stared at her, unsure of what to do. The children understood the precarious nature of their parents' relationship and understood their father wanted to keep them together as a family. Because of this unwritten rule, they hesitated.

Little Charlene said, "But Daddy's gone."

Then Mave said in a much sterner voice, "I said get in the car. You're gonna spend some time with yer mama." She knocked on the Henriksens' door, and her mother-in-law answered.

Mave said, "I'm spendin' sometime with the kids. Tell Gus he's welcome to come over if he wants."

"Well, all right," Mrs. Henriksen answered, surprised to see Mave.

At home, the kids feasted on the meal Mave prepared from scratch. Three hours into the visit, Charlene regaled everyone about how she almost replicated the cherry pie her mom made earlier that year, and then Gus walked in through screened kitchen door. The kids looked sheepishly at him while helping themselves to a second serving of the pound cake.

Sensing the discussion might get heated, Mave said, "Me and the kids ate. You're welcome to have some if you want, but the kids are stayin' with me tonight." She pointed to the door, and they both walked out.

"Gus, I love you. Come home," she said in earnest. "I don't need anythin' more in this world'n you. Please stay." This time Mave skipped the makeover and she appeared as Gus always loved her—as herself.

"What about school?" he asked.

"I'll go when Charlene's gone. I can go any time after that. Please. I love you. Come home."

It was a start. Gus moved back in with his wife and talked to her about how he felt about her in the marriage. He finally told the truth of what happened the night she got pregnant. At first Mave was extremely angry, and then she also opened up herself, letting Gus know exactly how she felt about what happened to them when they were kids. Months into their reconciliation, Mave gave Gus back his wedding ring.

"I've been holding onto this for you," she said one morning as he got himself ready for work. Gus slid the ring on, kissed his wife, grabbed his sack lunch, and headed out the door.

Chapter Fifty—A Far-off Place Called Home

Shirley completed her twentieth year in the service. She did not reenlist because she was ready to come home. Shirley arrived home in a much different manner than she left all those years ago. Her vehicle packed tightly with all her belongings, she pulled into the Carmichael property and looked for her parents. Daddy was taking care of family business in town, and Mama was in the yard feeding the chickens.

"You home for good this time, gal?" her mother asked. Shirley nodded as her mother slid her hand across the side of Shirley's head, soothing the fly-away hairs on her flaxen ponytail.

Before her interview with the Carter and Carter Research Institute, Shirley had the opportunity to spend time in town. She drove by the old candy store and saw McDonald's in its place. She drove further into town to the high school. Over the years, she thought about what would have become of her had she married Duck. The day after the two of them were engaged they came out to the high school, and she told him of her misgivings and her worries, and he promised to be a good husband to her. Even so, this promise was not enough, not enough to secure Shirley's hand in marriage.

The high school she attended was small in comparison to the building that stood before her. The city council had the auditorium and main building completely refurbished. She double backed and went by the church, where she sat under the awning. She reflected on how she and Mave, as girls, used to play under the foliage in the front, waiting for their parents to finish up whatever conversation they had started. The massive lot before her did not seem so large now. In fact, Shirley felt a little closed in and closed off. This feeling began when she settled into her old room at home. The house, in her previous visits, had been alive with her younger siblings, but now that everyone had grown, the house held a silence she was not used to. She went to the backyard but still found she could not escape this feeling, and then she called Mave.

"Shirley, is that you?" Mave asked.

"Yep."

"I wondered if you'd ever get around to calling me."

"I know. I need a favor."

"Is everything all right?"

"Yep. I just need a place to stay for a coupla days, possibly a week to two weeks." Shirley continued. "I've got this interview in Macon, and there are a coupla things I need to take care of before then."

"Do you plan on movin' out this way?"

"I dunno."

"While I've got you on the phone, guess who Gus bumped into?" Mave asked. Shirley waited on the other end for Mave to answer her own question.

"Guess. Well, okay, Jamie. He bumped into Jamie."

"Jamie," Shirley said slowly. She had not heard that name in years. Somewhere in between her living and his living they lost contact. "What's he doin'?"

"He's by himself. He's opened up a feedstore—" As Shirley listened to Mave, she became lost in thought about the missing years that separated her from Jamie. Then, as soon as that thought surfaced, she recalled Ms. Charmaine and the suit.

She tried on the suit Ms. Charmaine had given her almost twenty years earlier and found, while she still maintained a healthy physique, she had the body of a woman. The suit was a little snug in some places. When she and Mave arrived in Macon, they stopped for lunch, and then headed to the little storefront that had been Ms. Charmaine's Fine Silks and Garments. Shirley discovered Ms. Charmaine had moved into the business district downtown. She and Mave headed to the shop where they found Ms. Charmaine working diligently on an evening dress. Her new place of business was more upscale than her previous shop. She walked into the store, leaving Mave in the car.

"Is Ms. Charmaine in?" Shirley inquired of the girl taking orders by the cash register.

"Yes, can I ask who's asking?"

"Shirley Carmichael. I'm here to see if I can get something adjusted."

"One minute." The girl went toward the back to retrieve her boss. A few minutes later, Ms. Charmaine appeared, a little older, but the same old Ms. Charmaine.

"Hi darlin'. How you been?" Ms. Charmaine said, taking in the visual of the new Shirley and reflecting on the slip of the girl that left Macon almost twenty years ago.

"Hi, Ms. Charmaine, I'm fine. How's everything with you?"

"Well, it's going great. You see the shop," Ms. Charmaine said and gave Shirley a tour of the business. Ms. Charmaine managed to do wonders in the years Shirley had been gone. The place had a waiting room where her clients could help themselves to anything in the self-service fridge. The office sat in between a hair salon and a spa.

When the tour was complete, Shirley said, "I've got'n interview, but I need some alterations to this suit." Ms. Charmaine took Shirley back to the fitting room where Shirley changed into the snug suit.

"There's enough material here to make adjustments. Sit still for a minute."

While standing as Ms. Charmaine made marks in places with chalk by adding stickpins in other parts of the suit, Shirley thought to herself this was a perfect time to ask about her friend.

"How's Jamie?"

"Oh, he's fine. He's right outside of Macon."

"What's he doin'?"

"He and his father, because I don't know if you remember his father had a feed business, but he and his father run a feed business here in town."

"Yeah?"

"He's doin' fine." Ms. Charmaine said. She then continued, "That's about it. Be careful when you take that suit off. You don't want to get stuck."

Shirley stepped down off the small stool that Ms. Charmaine had her stand on to make the adjustments in the suit. Ms. Charmaine took Shirley's number and told her she would call when the item was ready. When she got back in the car, Mave was on her way back from perusing the district.

Headed home, they both sat quietly contemplating their lives until Mave asked, "That's Jamie's aunt?"

"Yeah. She's real nice lady."

"That's the one you stayed with when you left."

"Yep. I worked in the store too. That suit I took in for adjustments she made for me before I left for basic."

They sat quietly and then out of the blue, Mave asked, "Why didn't you and Jamie ever date?"

"He was cute, I guess, but I don't really think I was Jamie's type. Plus I hadn't outgrown my childhood fear of boys."

"What?" Mave asked and chuckled. "Sweetheart, what were you afraid of?"

"I don't know. They just always seemed to be chasing me with something, a worm, a frog, or something gross, and I just was scared of them, much less letting them kiss me." They both laughed.

"The way he would dote on you," Mave said, and then she added, "I guess we always end where we begin."

"We went to Homecoming together," Shirley said, leaving the statement hanging in the air, "but Jamie's a different sort." Shirley never considered Jamie to be more than a good friend. She wondered over the years how life had treated him. The last time she heard he was still married to Francesca.

When they returned to Mave's house, Shirley spent the rest of her time actually enjoying the visit. Something in Mave had changed and, to Shirley, her friend seemed quite happy. The years apart etched in each woman maturity and patience for each other. While the conversation may have changed from high school personal dramas to career plans and family, the girls were the same girls.

Ms. Charmaine called two days before the interview. Shirley drove her Volkswagen bug to the district. She had not really noticed the pick-up truck sitting in one of the metered parking lots as she entered the shop. In the shop, Jamie Wilkerson sat in Ms. Charmaine's waiting room.

She noticed the sandy crew cut that he kept closely cropped was changing on the sides to a golden-silver color. He wore the typical gear of a man from the South. This time, the difference was that he was relaxed.

"Well hello, stranger," Shirley said taking him all in.

"My aunt said you were inquiring about me, so I thought I'd just come show you myself," he said.

Shirley smiled a wide grin and sat next to her old friend, where he regaled her with his adventures of love and life.

Chapter Fifty-one—May 1985

Sitting under the oak tree with Mave and her now-grown daughters, Shirley marvels at the revolution both of their lives have taken. The women converse about a time long ago. The hot afternoon settling into a calm dusk, the women watch as the men finish erecting the tents in yet another May evening wedding reception. When the last tent has been put up, the men come over to retrieve their wives, girlfriends, and dates. Gus, a forty-three-year-old grandfather, takes an already-standing Mave to the dance area. Not to be forgotten, Jamie leads Shirley by the hand in what would be one of the many dances the two would share as a married couple.

Epilogue: Eleven

"You'll think you'll ever get married, Shirley?"

Eleven-year-old Mave and Shirley sat under the church awning contemplating one Sunday in the Georgia heat what to do now that they were no longer required to keep the church clothes clean while the ice lollies they enjoyed melted all over their dresses.

"I don't know, Maverick, seems like a lot of work."

"Yeah, I'm with you. Let's see if the boys want to play tag."

"Lets."

www.ingramcontent.com/pod-product-compliance
Lightning Source LLC
Chambersburg PA
CBHW021221130626
46554CB00004B/1313